Don't you know who I used to be?

from manolos to motherhood...

JULIA MORRIS

hachette
AUSTRALIA

Published in Australia and New Zealand in 2009
by Hachette Australia
(An imprint of Hachette Australia Pty Limited)
Level 17, 207 Kent Street, Sydney NSW 2000
www.hachette.com.au

National Library of Australia
Cataloguing-in-Publication data

Morris, Julia.
Don't you know who I used to be? / Julia Morris.

1st ed.

978 0 7336 2390 5 (pbk.)

Morris, Julia.

Women comedians--Australia--Biography.

792.7028092

Cover design by Christabella Designs
Cover photographs of Julia © Sean Izzard Photography
www.seanizzard.com
Cover photograph of baby courtesy of istock photography
Text design by Bookhouse, Sydney
Typeset in Adobe Garamond Pro
Printed in Australia by Griffin Press, Adelaide

Hachette Australia's policy is to use papers that are natural, renewable and recyclable products and made from wood grown in sustainable forests. The logging and manufacturing processes are expected to conform to the environmental regulations of the country of origin.

To my beautiful Thomases, Dan, Ruby and Sophie,
I was lost without you.

Jx

1

Rule Britannia

When your life is about to change forever, you'd think there would be a more significant marker. But in my case there wasn't. There was just me wondering, is that a line or a cross?

Okay, so it turned out it was a cross, but did the cross mean pregnant or did the line? I seriously had no idea. The tests I had used in the past at least had the decency to actually say **NOT PREGNANT**. You'd think that weeing on a stick (and most of my hand) would be the most humiliating part of this whole exercise, but it wasn't. Going into the chemist to buy the test was even more hideous.

At the start of that day in March 2006, I had no idea what was about to happen. I had been shooting in Kings Cross with a team of extraordinarily fabulous gay men in what is commonly described in the industry as a 'film taster'. Hmmm, maybe some of that sentence needs clarifying. Firstly, I assume you know that 'shooting' is fancy talk for filming . . . with so many actual shootings going on over the years in Sydney's famous Kings Cross, I think it is always best to check. Secondly, hello, *fabulous gay men in Sydney*, what a shock. The fabulous goes without saying. And, thirdly, the 'film taster'.

Now, the TV and film industries have been in such a strange financial state over the past ten years that they have become way too conservative in their programming and as a result it has been increasingly difficult to get anything commissioned that doesn't generate its own income. Fewer films and TV shows are being made so every level of the industry is suffering.

Many commissioning executives are (rightly) scared of making a flop and losing their jobs, so most of them stick to very safe formats – terrible news for comedians. As a result nothing gets made or even gets a meeting without a taster.

The 'taster' is usually funded by what is left in the writer's bank account after food and rent so, of course, he or she then begs for the help of industry friends to put together something that will ultimately not be picked up due to the lower production quality rather than the overall concept.

Loads of industry people are willing to work on the taster on the off-chance that the film or show gets picked up and a job might be on offer.

The writer of this particular film was a hurtfully talented man I had met years before at Comedy Camp, a gay comedy club in London's Soho. Back then, after a few post-show mojitos at Balans on Old Compton Street, he and I had agreed to launch into a long-distance homosexual/gay man-meets-woman-in-Ming-Blue-Jimmy-Choos-let's-speak-on-the phone-once-a-month type of relationship, with me living in London and him moving home to Sydney. He would ring and tell me of his script developments and in return I giggled and heckled. So when he found out I was coming home to Australia for my annual month-long stand-up tour, he was determined to get a cast of friends together and shoot the taster.

As I left the hotel I knew I was in for a great day, as filming with gay men is always way too much fun. As well as an über-hip crew, you are always guaranteed exceptionally good coffee served by some lickable 19-year-old trying to get into the entertainment industry by not wearing a shirt, which I have to tell you is just fine with me. I'd dressed to impress in a hot-pink Miu Miu shift and gravity-defying Liberty-print Gina heels. I'd gone for a slice-of-summer-heaven look but the only thing the crew could talk about was how big and fabulously high my hooters were.

It's difficult to describe how intensely satisfying it is even to get a homosexual/gay man to look at you, much less comment on a part of the anatomy that, quite frankly, they have had little to do with since they were babies. 'Honey, your tits look fabulous in that dress,' the lighting director said. I just smiled and lifted them a little higher.

It was only when I was in the cab on the way home that I looked down and realised my boobs were looking bigger than usual. It started me thinking. I pulled a diary out of my bag and looked for the day a month before marked with a very discreet 'P'.

Oh . . . my . . . God. Thirty days ago. Thirty! Surely not. I asked the cab driver to stop (and you know how accommodating they can be) at a chemist on Oxford Street and I ran in. Now, why is it that chemists only seem to stock pregnancy tests that look like they were made in the late '70s? And then they hide them to make sure you have to ask where they are. If you pick one up and go through the checkout at a supermarket no one raises an eyebrow, but at the chemist every employee is obviously trained to give you some instruction on how to use the **PREGNANCY TEST** at the top of their voice (I know I sound like some sort of pregnancy test regular and should take home a Campbell's Cash and Carry slab of them . . . but you don't get to 38 without having to do one or two along the way).

I was just getting ready to die while listening to the pimply 16-year-old shop assistant explain loudly how the stick should be placed mid-stream when my favourite thing happened. The other assistant bellowed, 'Didn't you used to be that girl on TV?' I just nodded as the sheer mortification of having everyone turn around and give me the judgemental 'dirty' stare, like I was the only one 'doing it', overwhelmed me. I handed over the money and did the walk of whorey shame out of the shop, trying to make sure as many people as possible could see my wedding ring.

The cab driver had been thrilled to wait, so sped all the way to the hotel to make up time. Running straight into the bathroom, I followed the chemist assistant's instructions and waited the advised time. Now, I had seen the 'yes' cross before, so seeing the 'yes' cross this day made me feel a little uneasy. (But this was no time to dwell on disasters of ectopic proportions.) At the same time, I also felt weirdly calm and proud. But like anyone who has lost a baby in the very early stages, I didn't want to get too excited . . . just in case.

I was in such a rush to do that test that I'd arrived back at the hotel suite without saying anything to my husband, Dan. Dan is not just my husband, he is my very best friend. The one person I can't wait to speak to whenever anything happens – and I mean anything. I might have dropped some icing sugar down my shirt and I am straight on the phone. So you can imagine the look on his face when I bounded into the loungeroom and with absolutely no warning signals (like 'I'm late' or 'Hey, I stopped to pick up a pregnancy test') I just blurted out of nowhere, 'Oh my God, I am totally knocked up!' He looked shocked, happy, and just a little terrified.

To say the rest of the stand-up tour was gruelling would be an understatement. Once the excitement wore off, I still had 15 shows left to play up and down the east coast of Australia. I was so very tired and had no idea that I was in the early stages of pregnancy anaemia. There are worse things, I know, but it was certainly a challenge to get onto a stage at 10 o'clock at night and use more than a day's energy to entertain a crowd. When I wasn't travelling to the next gig I took up residence on whatever couch was around and made sure the TV remote and chocolate were close . . . bliss.

I always think it sounds really chic to be 'on tour'. I love saying 'on tour'. Saying, 'Yeah, I'm on tour right now' makes me feel like Elton John or Willie Nelson. Not that Elton or Willie ever had to tour with pregnancy anaemia ('On the road again, taking iron tablets on the road again . . .'). That doesn't sound so glamorous. The truth is, touring is the life of a comedian. You are never really not on tour. If you're not on tour you don't eat, it's that simple. There are only so many nights you can perform at the Canterbury/Hurlstone Park RSL, so there is the need to keep moving to a new audience. You have to go further afield. That's why I'd moved to the UK in the first place.

But if I am completely honest there were other reasons to move. It was late 1999 and my television work was drying up. Reality television was on the rise and apart from appearing on two episodes a fortnight of *Beauty and the Beast* (and being called an idiot by my dear mate Stan Zemanek, which, let's face it, does have a certain level of truth to it), there was very little else around. Sadly, the only other TV offers coming my way were hosting shows like *Australia's Greatest Pet Headstands* or *Battle of the Printers, The Untold Story.* It wasn't the sort of work that was going to satisfy me.

The problem was, I had been very spoilt up until then. When I was 22 I started compering eight shows a week at the Comedy Store in Sydney. In 1994 I was 'discovered' by Doug McLeod, the head writer and a producer on the Channel 7 comedy sketch show *Full Frontal.* He saw me in a stand-up club in Balmain and asked me to fly to Melbourne to audition for his show. I was lucky enough to get in. Two years later, I was headhunted by Channel 9 to work on their variety show *In Melbourne Tonight* with Frankie J. Holden, Denise Drysdale and the delicious Steven Jacobs. The whole time I moonlighted with Foxtel on Stan's *Beauty and the Beast* and then in 1998 I leapt to Channel 10. Nothing like being versatile and covering nearly all the bases.

It was not just in the television world that I was approaching my use-by date. I was a 32-year-old woman with no boyfriend, in fact, I didn't even have a crush on anyone. Most of my friends were married and starting the whole baby thing and they kept asking me when I was going to settle down. How much did I love being asked that question? How about when I meet someone. I am not going to wait all that time till my thirties and then just lock it down with any moron. 'The one' was going to have to be pretty spectacular as my list of wants and needs was getting longer. I was beginning to think I was going to have to face life on some sort of shelf. I was ready for some big changes.

For a long time I had dreamed of working in the UK but never had the guts to leave everything behind to do it. My grandmother hadn't been naturalised in Australia so I had an Irish passport. And, as far as I am concerned, Britain is the comedy capital of the planet, where all the best comedies I had ever really loved were made. So, after braving the Edinburgh Festival in 1999, I decided I would move there, do some writing, maybe a bit of stand-up and within a few months I would surely have my own show. Easy!

I could not have been more wrong. The thing is, Aussies are not such a novelty in the UK any more. We have been heavily invading the shores of Britain since the mid-60s and there are over 300 000 Australians now living in London. My fresh voice was not as fresh, or as wanted, as I'd hoped it would be.

I arrived at Heathrow on 25 May 2000 and immediately lobbed in on some incredibly stylish dear friends in their maxi-glam, open-plan, double-income-no-kids pad in Wapping in East London, right on the Thames. It was more luxury than I knew what to do with. I'd been told that life in London could be really hard, but during those first few weeks I decided that was just so not true. I was being kept like King Farouk and loving it. It couldn't last forever . . . and didn't. The moment came for me to spread my wings and find an apartment of my own.

It was reality check time. Did I say apartment? It was most definitely a flat! I had been having such a glorious time with my kind friends but I had stepped into their lives and left mine behind. So when it came time to move I got a very real taste of what it was like to be a single woman, without a job, in London.

Work-wise, no one cared what sort of experience I had. No amount of television credits or show reels could get me through the doors of anywhere. I had to start my career from scratch. I had to show up to the open-mike amateur nights and give it a go! Have you ever heard the song from *Sesame Street* that says 'One of these things is not like the other'? Well, all the other open-mike performers were either beginners, students or nutters. I was a 32-year-old woman with 11 years of stand-up experience and a bad taste in my mouth from all the humble pie I was having to consume. Not to mention I was the only comic in Gucci sling-backs and a La Perla diamante slip. Surely someone had to book me, hello?

I spent the first three months doing free shows. I made my way across the UK performing in clubs for FREE so they could assess whether or not I was good enough to be paid to work in their club. I trekked from Brighton to Cardiff, from Birmingham to Manchester, from Leeds to Newcastle, and from Blackpool to Glasgow using my own money to try to get a start. It was very different to ringing up a comedy club in Australia and speaking to the owner, someone I'd probably known for years, and asking if I could do a set. This was a whole new ball game and it was very draining on so many different levels. Even if the clubs loved me, there would inevitably be no slots available for ages, as all comics are booked at least six months in advance.

In the year before I left Australia I had worked like a slave and managed to save about $22 000, which I thought was a fortune. It wasn't. Four months of travel, rent and fees for my second month-long festival in Edinburgh meant I had gone through the lot by the end of August 2000. I returned to London in what is commonly known as dire straits. Never really having experienced the 'hand to mouth' existence before, I found being broke extremely confronting.

I was struggling and started to think I'd made a big mistake leaving Australia. I reached my lowest point on the opening night of the Sydney Olympics.

Perched in my little flat in North London, eating tuna and Ryvitas for brekkie (a superbly cheap meal) for about the 18th day in a row, I flicked on the TV and on came Sydney's Opening Ceremony. It was about 10am and I cheered as each country's team made its way into the stadium. (Especially East Timor, remember how they danced with such joy? What champions!) I don't know why it affected me so strongly but I starting sobbing a deep guttural sob that I have never experienced before or since. Hitting a crescendo of howling during Vanessa Amorosi's 'Heroes Live Forever' as a massive flag of projected images of triumphant Olympians rose up and over the crowd, I was a mess. I seriously thought I should just pack it in and go home. But then my ego kicked in. What about all the stories I did in magazines before I left on how I was going to make my fame and fortune? And all the farewell parties and the big send-off? I would just look like a liar and a failed liar at that.

The shame of it, coupled with an intense homesickness and the fact that on the other side of the world, somewhere in that opening night crowd of people at Homebush, were my mum, my dad and my brother. It was sending me into dark hysterics. I didn't think I could take any more and, despite the risk to my ego, I was starting to plan the flight home when, all of a sudden, there was a hitch in the broadcast. Our goddess Cathy Freeman had walked up to a raised platform wearing an all-in-one white leotard (I am sorry but who looks good in white Lycra? The woman *is* a goddess). She lit the mini torch that was supposed to rise up to trigger the main cauldron but it refused to rise. It just wouldn't start moving. Still not moving. Cathy was just standing there and it was still not moving. The thing was so not moving, just shaking a little. Well, I started laughing. Laughing and laughing and laughing. I kept thinking that this was so Australian. I had visions of the technicians saying, 'Nah, don't worry about testing it, she'll be right on the night.' And then it rose. Triumphant over all. Something shifted in me at that point. I'd needed to take a good long hard look at myself and then snap out of it. I was living the opportunity of a lifetime. New country, new start, new chance to leave the shackles of the past and emerge like a Phoenix from the flames of my misery (okay . . . maybe that is too much, but you get the idea). It was time to stop feeling sorry for myself and let my own 'emotional torch' rise.

Not long after the Olympics things slowly started to change. Not in a huge Hallmark life-is-now-fabulous-after-hitting-rock-bottom way. But enough for me to stay. I got my first paid show in a venue in North London's famously grungy Camden. The venue was part of a big chain of comedy clubs called Jongleurs, so doing well at the Camden club meant lots of work around the country and decent pay, which was of course the main drawcard. The room could normally hold about 400 audience members but this night was special as England was playing in the Euro 2000 soccer competition – most of the nation were in pubs watching the game which was on at the same time I was performing. The only people who weren't watching the game were the 15 people at my show, seven of whom had been dragged in kicking and screaming by their wives, so no hostility there, and my brand-new British agent. The compere was very nice to me backstage, making me feel welcome with a drink and offering me a puff of his jazz ciggie, which I politely declined.

The biggest highlight of the night came when the compere introduced me. Appealing to the already silent 'crowd', he said, 'The next act is Australian and it's a girl so no guarantees that she will be funny, but she does give a great blow job. Please welcome Julia Roberts.' Excellent. Yes. Good. Thank you. 'So nice to be here.' I think it is safe to say the gig did not go as well as I had hoped. I was only one story into my act when one of the staff ran into the room and yelled, 'Oh my God, Shearer just scored a goal!' At the time I had no idea what that meant but the room cleared, leaving only my agent in her seat. Everyone else ran up to the back of the club to watch the replay on the television behind the bar. My agent called out from her seat that Shearer was in fact Alan Shearer, the captain of the English team and his goal meant that England would now move through to the quarter finals. I could not have been more pleased for them.

The next few shows weren't much better, but at least I was being paid. It took me quite a while to learn the age-old lesson that you have to live in a city for about 30 years before you are allowed to complain about anything. To complain as a newly arrived Australian was just not on. I was still in the infamous first-six-months-of-living-in-London head-space of how Australia is the best place on the planet and how Britain never sees the sun, *blah blah blah*. Even in Australia, as soon as someone complains about our country, we tend to say, 'Why don't you just piss off back to where you came from.' Well, not surprisingly, that is the exact reaction I got while making my comedy observations about what a tough city London was. I pointed out how weird all the black stuff that collects in your nose when you ride the tube was and how aggressive everyone seemed to be. Nobody wanted to hear it. The natural local reaction was to tell me to f*%$ off back to where I came from. The irony was, of course, that this *was* the land of my ancestors, so I had and I was still not welcome.

Though they didn't like to hear my observations about their homeland, most of the British people I met in those first few months wanted to share with me all their observations on the history of mine . . . how we were all convict, colonial stock. I swear, if I heard one more Cockney ask me if it was still necessary to steal a loaf of bread to get to Australia I was going to start throwing punches. Here is what I could pick up from their many pissed lectures . . . Apparently about 220-odd years ago the government in the UK found some really naughty people. Some of them had stolen some bread and others had read the wrong books. To get rid of this disgusting element out of the UK (which totally worked cause it is *sooo* classy now) they put them onto a boat and to really punish them sent them off to the other side of the planet. They did stop off in South Africa first, where they said, 'We will be back to kill you later.' The English must have been a lot of fun in those days – they just went from place to place killing people, well, those they didn't rape, actually they probably killed them too. I guess I wasn't there so I can hardly judge.

Well, then they got back onto the boat and it sailed all the way around Australia and dropped the prisoners off in Sydney, at Bennelong Point. By the end of the 100th history lesson I was almost ready to head back to Bennelong myself. Though despite my colonial heritage that area is forever linked to opals and Ugh boots in my mind. But that is another story.

One step forward, two steps back. That's how I felt living in the UK. Besides trying to find some comedic common ground I was also trying to get used to my new position in the showbiz pecking order. Welcome to the bottom shelf, population: me.

There was one bright light at the end of the tunnel, though. I had been spotted by BBC news journalist and television host Christopher Price during the Edinburgh Festival, after being a part of a Channel 4 documentary called *Edinburgh or Bust*. The doco followed four comedians hoping to make a splash at the festival, which is no mean feat considering there are more than 3500 performers in venues varying from

2000-seat arenas to laundromat basements seating 30. There was even one gig in a lift that allowed five audience members. The festival is so diverse, with performers coming from all over the globe, and it is way too much fun for someone who loves a night out, like me.

Fortunes can be made and lost at the Edinburgh Festival and any unknown performer is hostage to the newspaper reviews that can kick you into or out of the spotlight. (Well, reviews and how much time you spend on the famous Royal Mile with the *huuuumiliating* task of trying to sell your show by handing out flyers on the street in an interesting way in competition with the other 3499 performers.) That year I was sharing my show with an American comedian named Karen Loftus, who was loads of fun and an excellent late-night partner in drinking-crime. It is safe to say that at times we were more concerned with where the parties were than with the show, but somehow we still managed to get superb reviews. Amazing what many cans of Red Bull and quite a few headache tablets can do.

Thanks to the festival, slowly my phone started ringing. Christopher Price, who was now hosting a show on the BBC called *Liquid News*, called and asked me if I would come on as a guest pundit. (I had never heard the word pundit before but apparently it's a smart-arse who thinks they know everything about everything. I was bound to fit right in.) I thought I was in heaven. My appearance meant my first time on the hallowed turf that is BBC Television Centre. For me Television Centre is a shrine and the home to every show that I have ever loved. From *Brideshead* to *Parky*, from *To the Manor Born* to *Absolutely Fabulous*, it was as we say in my home town of Gosford, the duck's nuts. Was this how Hillary felt when he started his mammoth climb up Everest? Was this how Crusoe felt seeing a ship just off shore? Was this how . . . well, you get the picture. I felt like I was filled with a power so much greater than me and I was being chauffeur-driven directly to the door. Oh my God . . . I had made it.

Liquid News was quite unlike anything I had worked on before. It was clever, funny and so incredibly of the moment. It was an informative chat show but also a wonderful piss-take on modern society's obsession with celebrity rolled up in a daily news format. As much as I love celebrity news culture I also loathe it and Christopher felt the same way so we fell instantly in love. He was a high-profile, classy and understated gay man and I was an old fruit fly from way back, so as if we weren't going to fall. He was mad for my shoes and I was insane for the way he constructed his sentences. (Earlier I snuck in a homage to Christopher with the phrase homosexual/gay. It was an expression he dropped with reckless abandon and I looooved it. Not just gay but homosexual gay, so much leather, so few saddles. Just the best.)

My fellow guest that first episode was a chap named Lemmy from a band called Motorhead. Now, I am not very groovy and I had no idea who Lemmy was but I knew from his stovepipe jeans, Cuban cowhide heels and 'total eclipse of the heart' midnight-black hairdo, that he must have been some sort of a rocker. Correct. In fact he rocked so hard that when he was told he could not have a cigarette on air, as we were on BBC premises, he stormed off the set and out into the night, leaving Christopher and I to chitty-chat about the day's celebrity news during what should have been Lemmy's airtime. It just couldn't get any better. I went home that night feeling like I was finally getting back a little slice of my old Australian life with a Britannia twist. I liked it and thought I just might hang around awhile.

I cannot give enough thanks that I did hang around. Without taking that initial leap into the unknown and moving to the UK in the first place, I would never have set the series of events in motion that led to me meeting and marrying Dan and, now, thanks to a blue cross on a stick we had our fingers crossed we were about to have a baby.

2

What a Difference a Friend Makes

I wrote my first Logies speech when I was eight and living in Springfield on the New South Wales Central Coast. It basically was a thank you to my best friend Rebecca and dobbing in my nasty 3rd grade teacher Mrs Fry before doing a loungeroom-choreographed liturgical dance to KC and the Sunshine Band's 'Boogie Shoes'.

It was all Mum and Dad's 'fault'. They gave my brother and I so much love and support that we really thought we could do anything. Not that being an entertainer would have been among their first choices for me, knowing that it is a road filled with lots of heartache, but as long as I was happy they came to every concert, Christmas pageant and even poetry recitals at local eisteddfods (first prize for 'Mulga Bill's Bicycle').

Singing into the mirror in my bedroom when I was 17 gave me the idea of sending a letter to Bert Newton's *New Faces* to try to get on the show. Taking a day off school was easier for me than it was for most, as I commuted by train for just over an hour to Sydney . . . so slipping off to attend the audition went unnoticed. It wasn't until a letter arrived at our house from Channel 9 that my caper was blown wide open. I had been accepted to go to Melbourne to compete on the show but had to be accompanied by an adult. Let's just say Mum and Dad were not pleased that I had been dishonest and wagged school but they agreed to let me give it a go. Off we went for my first television experience. I ended up tying for first place with a girls' marching band. (Enough said.)

I would never have thought during that first trip, or even during my days as Calamity Jane with the Gosford Musical Society, that just over 15 years later

I would be living and working in London *almost* making a living in showbiz. Except for the 'hardly any money' bit, I was 'living the dream'.

By the end of 2000 the thought of babies was a *looooooooooong* way in my future. I was still working hard to establish myself and *Liquid News* had become a really important part of my nearly non-existent income. I was booked to appear on the show every fortnight but Christopher had become such a good work friend that he was including me in lots of the new ventures he was developing and hosting. Because of him, I was starting to feel like a real local at the 'Beeb' (BBC).

One of Christopher's new-year projects for 2001 had one of the best titles I have ever heard for a TV show . . . *Celebrity Roadkill.* It was a panel discussion/game show about celebrities and our love/hate relationship with all of the information we can access about them. Let's be honest, it is frightening how much many of us know about the lives of people we have never met. Details like what they are wearing, where they are eating, who they are dating, who they are fighting with, who has cellulite and who has just bought a pregnancy test (obviously tipped off by some chemist shop assistant). The paparazzi are more than happy to provide the product, the magazines are the dealers and we are the gossip junkies.

A good deal of our society seems to be stuck in the middle of some sort of celebrity information obsession, which is now playing out more like a bizarre reality show. We watch celebrities' lives unfold from afar and then feel compelled to comment with authority on even the most intimate details (think Britney Spears). The fact is, most of the 'information' we are fed is made up by some work experience journalist who is trying to fill column inches. The most disturbing part of all is . . . I just *LOVE* it. Long before *Celebrity Roadkill* came along I read those mags and stored that information. You can only imagine how delighted I was to be paid to do something I do anyway.

The producer I teamed up with during the development of the show was a heavenly Northern Irishman named Angus. Like a waft of his Creed-Green Irish

Tweed manfume, Angus was 'as refreshing as a walk through the Irish countryside, spicy and unforgettable'. (Also, like the description of the fragrance, he had been 'favoured through the years by some of Hollywood's leading men', but that's another story.) Years before, Angus had been the lead singer of a Belfast band called Slut Cupboard. I heard that and knew I had found a soul mate.

I think the moment we fell in friendship love was while filming at the *Esquire* Man of the Year ceremony. There was a hurtfully handsome cameraman from another production company who kept banging into our table and I said, 'If he does that one more time, he's going to have to get nude.' Angus replied that not only did he think that was an excellent idea but that he and I clearly had very similar views on a wide range of issues.

From that moment on, we became instant partners in showbiz-crime. Our daily grind consisted of writing feverishly at White City (the location of the BBC Television Centre) until knock-off time and then making our way into London's famous West End for a few dry white wines and maybe one or two canapés. It was during one of these drinking adventures that I slurringly confided in Angus how tough things had been financially for me since arriving in the UK and how super broke I was.

Even though I was living the dream and things were much brighter than they had been I was still broke. A few more work opportunities were coming in, but pilot show development is not the highest paid sector of the entertainment industry and I was still slogging away doing free gigs to build my name and reputation in the Motherland. My share of the rent was £200 a week (in 2001 more than AU$500) for a room the size of a postage stamp close to central London, so I would often face having to choose between booze or food. That night with Angus I'd chosen booze and as we all know *in vino veritas* ('there is truth in wine'), which explains my honesty about my financial state. Angus was so disturbed by my story that he made me go directly to an automatic teller machine with him. He took out £300 and gave it to me, saying, 'I don't care when or even if I get this back but someone gave me a similar cash break years ago and it really turned my luck around.'

I was so overcome by Angus's kindness (yes, there were drunk girly tears) and it turned out he was so right about the changing luck. *Celebrity Roadkill* was a great fun pilot episode (I wore a red and white Diane von Furstenberg classic crossover dress and red patent wedge Gucci heels that I had bought years before when I was still on Channel 9 wages), but sadly the show did not get commissioned to be a series. (Oh, my word, that almost never happens in TV . . . how I wish you could hear my sarcastic tone.)

What did come out of it, though, which I directly attribute to my 'Angus luck', was that I caught the eye of the world-renowned comedy guru, BBC executive producer Jon Plowman. Jon is responsible for such British all-time gems as *Absolutely Fabulous*, *French and Saunders*, *The Office*, *The League of Gentlemen*, *The Vicar of Dibley* and *Little Britain*, to name a few. Just about any comedy you have loved from the UK in the past 30 or so years will have Jon Plowman's name on it. So when he offered me a £2000 development deal to come up with a sitcom script to star in, I nearly split my spleen with the excitement.

I got straight on the phone to Angus and after many mutual squeals of disbelief, we made a very sensible plan. We would invest the money wisely by flying to somewhere on the Mediterranean and hiring a sensational yet rustic house so we could write solidly for two weeks. We had already thrown around a number of sitcom ideas on our nights out, so getting away from London and allowing them to flourish seemed like a no-brainer.

After doing some research into great writing locations on the Med, Angus came up with the Northern Cypriot village of Bellapais. It is perched up in the hills above the city of Kyrenia and is home to the Bellapais Abbey. Angus assured me it was going to be a calm and relaxing opportunity to work, be inspired and sample the Cyprus of the bygone era immortalised in the book *Bitter Lemons* by Lawrence Durrell. Early September in Bellapais was apparently the perfect month for long end-of-summer days, so we knew we were on a winner.

I'd seen pictures of where we were going but nothing prepared me for the feeling of the place. The sense of lives lived before was strong, and the Abbey itself seems to stand guard over the whole of the northern coastline. It was such a beautiful building. Apparently it is one of the most important Gothic buildings in the Near East. Very different from Erina Fair shopping centre, let me tell you!

Above the Abbey is the main part of the village, with tiny lanes and narrow streets that form almost a labyrinth around the main square. Whitewashed houses, a few restaurants and the odd bar circle around it. The house we rented belonged to a friend of Angus's, who had bought it in the late '60s. It was a massive, three-storey, rambling old gem that had views from every level over the plains of Kyrenia and straight out to the blinding azure blue of the glistening Mediterranean. We were hoping for views over some of the Turkish military-installation shower blocks but I'm old enough to know a girl can't have everything.

Just adjacent to our house was the famous mulberry Durrell wrote about, called the 'Tree of Idleness'.

Ancient folklore says that those seated beneath this famous tree become lazy and unwilling to work. Angus and I knew that was so not true . . . as long as working on your tan counts.

Once we'd made ourselves at home we committed to quite a busy workload in order to get the creative juices flowing. Our days went like this:

9am or 10am-ish	Get up and make breakfast enquiries
11am	Head to the beach
4pm–5pm	Brandy sours (two each) at the Abbey (thank God!). Glass of rosé, selection of paté, chorizo and haloumi, start work
6pm–8pm	Break open another bottle of local rosé and apply Aerogard, dinner time and mutual back-patting for brilliant ideas session
10.30pm	Bedtime

It was a gruelling timetable but we were determined and the work simply had to get done.

But seriously, apart from Angus and I starting to look like very relaxed film stars, we actually managed to get quite a lot of the scripts for six episodes completed. We wrote the characters with specific comic actors in mind and the storylines reflected the cultural differences between urban Britain and modern Australia (something I was more than acquainted with). It was loads of fun; we even added a cute whippet dog named Mrs Simpson who slept on an ornate, miniature Louis XVI love seat covered with Beauvais tapestry and growled every time she saw an image or footage of the Queen Mother. (We laughed for hours about Mrs Simpson and her gin-soaked ermine off-cuts.)

Inevitably, after such intense work hours and great results we both felt the need to get away from our scene of feverish intellectual intensity. I think this was about four days after we had arrived. So we jumped in our beep-beep type of open-top jeep and headed about an hour and a half north-east to the Karpas Peninsula which, owing to its shape, is more commonly referred to as the 'pan handle'.

I wonder if this is the place where God goes on holidays. With its golden beaches that stretch for miles and miles with barely a soul in sight and the magnificent views, you almost miss the smorgasbord of Byzantine churches, Neolithic remains and Bronze Age settlements. I have to say, though, as mad as I am for a bit of old stuff, I got just as excited about the local farmers. That first day I saw them all making their way to have an afternoon beverage, trying to avoid a couple of wild donkeys, on a tractor! (The local farmers were on tractors, not the donkeys . . . although never say never.)

Wanting to sample some of the local grape on the Peninsula, we decided to park ourselves overnight in a couple of beach huts on stilts just near the Monastery of Apostolos Andreas. It was fabulous travelling with Angus because we were both on the same wavelength. I was a mostly single woman in her sexual prime, so to speak, hoping the only thing separating me from one of the heaving, muscular local men would be a sheet. Angus was thinking the exact same thing.

Sadly, neither of us went to bed with more than the sheet.

At least we were fresh and alert for our next day's sightseeing. This was not a religious pilgrimage but we did spend a lot of time going from abbeys to monasteries (thank God we weren't struck down in any of them). Being from a country where the oldest National Trust protected houses are about 220 years old, it blew my tiny mind.

We learned that Saint Andrew had briefly landed in Cyprus on his final missionary journey back to his Palestinian homeland. While there he managed to reveal a spring whose waters miraculously healed the blind captain of his ship. In a strange and uncanny coincidence, Angus and I were also temporarily blinded and that very same spring water was the only thing that seemed to restore our sight the next day. Mmm, I know, it's really deep.

Minibreak over, it was time to get back to work. The drive back to our base was filled with long, narrow winding roads that made us both feel a little on edge. That was when I got the weirdest text message from a guy I know. It read 'New York City – Kaboom!' It made no sense and Angus and I both found it really strange and disturbing. We were a long way from anywhere, which reinforced the foreboding that crept over me. I was worried that something bad had happened but I had no idea what. We stopped and tuned into BBC World radio, just to put our minds at ease. We were little prepared for what we heard. I remember a panel of people speaking in frightened, solemn tones. They were saying things like: 'Never in the history of America has there ever been such a disaster,' and 'Today will be the last time we feel safe in New York,' and 'It's the sheer scale of this tragedy that makes it all the more incomprehensible.'

No one was saying what had happened exactly. It was bizarre. We were both shaking our heads saying, 'But what is *it*?' The rest of our drive seemed to take forever and the radio drifted in and out of reception. We were thinking, earthquake? Bomb? What?

When we arrived back in Bellapais we headed straight into a bar. It seemed like the whole town had gathered there to watch Turkish CNN on the bar television. It was here I saw for the first time the images that are now seared into my consciousness. I watched disbelievingly as the two planes sliced through the twin towers of the World Trade Center. Both buildings were on fire in the live coverage.

Watching such shocking footage with the commentary in another language made it even harder to comprehend what had happened. I assumed it had been an aviation disaster and I still had no idea terrorism was involved. Angus and I sat in that bar and drank brandy sours trying to decipher exactly what was going on. We were sitting there as the towers collapsed. It didn't seem real. I felt like I was watching a Will Smith film. I *wanted* to be watching a Will Smith film. An overwhelming feeling of dread had settled over everyone in the bar as we realised how many people must have died in the collapse. I had only been in the twin towers two years before and, even now, as I recall that day I still can't really believe it happened.

We had no television in the house, so for days, thirsty for more information, we would sit in the car listening to BBC World radio for any updates. It felt, as Jimmy Barnes would say, like we were standing on the outside looking in.

The little internet café in the village was overflowing and our email inboxes were bombarded by friends and family telling us to get back home as soon as possible. The Turkish military, which were always very visible in the streets of the village, had grouped at the airstrips and bases getting ready to mobilise. Even though we were a long way from home Angus and I were in no rush to get back to London. We felt safe so far away from anywhere.

At that point we had nine days left of our 'work camp' and decided not to hurry back to the UK. If this was going to turn into Armageddon, we reckoned we were better lying down in the Cypriot sun. So we did. Stop (afternoon nap), Revive (rosé), Survive (double-cream brie). It seemed like the sensible way forward.

When we returned to a very sombre London every newspaper reported imminent war stories and people were generally distracted, tentative and almost visibly scared. The strange thing about working in a field like comedy is that in tough times our business is at its busiest. People needed a bit of escapism through laughter, so venues all over town were full every night.

Angus and I submitted our sitcom scripts and went back to our respective 'day jobs', his at the BBC and mine out in stand-up clubs all around the country. (We are expecting feedback on the scripts any day now . . .)

Just before leaving for Cyprus I had spent the entire month of August in Edinburgh for my third festival, doing a one-woman show called 'Show and Tell'. It was an hour-long set of blistering-pace stand-up where I did more telling than showing. Edinburgh is such a wild place to be during festival time. The bonus is that if your show is selling out and you are socialising, well, drinking, every night till late enough, then you have the opportunity to meet all sorts of contacts who could potentially bring you work. That year I made buddies with a few casting women from the BBC and so when I returned from Cyprus there were a few casting calls waiting for me.

I hadn't been *too* wild in Edinburgh as I was seeing a ridiculously handsome Aussie boy at the time. All my comic friends nicknamed him 'Superman' but when Angus and I got home from Cyprus he dumped me by text message . . . so maybe not so super after all. I think it took me at least two or three days to get over him. Luckily, I could throw myself into work.

Going to castings (or auditions, as the kids from *Fame* called them) is a nerve-wracking experience at the best of times. Of course every casting call is different but generally you want to arrive at the audition with one 'bit of business' (a small anecdote that doesn't take up too much time and shows off a whisper of your personality). You will find this hard to believe, but I get a little overexcited and want to make the whole room laugh, so my auditions end up turning into mini gigs. It always amazed me that I would run out of time and hardly have a moment to focus on the script I had come in for.

For me, auditions end up feeling like so many dates I had been on. They are great at the time, whoever I am with laughs heartily, but they never call back. *Boo hoo*. Two castings that did pay off just before the Christmas of that year were *Chambers* and *Happiness*. *Chambers* was a very grown up comedy on BBC One starring John Bird and James Fleet, about the legal chambers of some very confused barristers (it's the sort of comedy that is often actually too intelligent for me to watch). I got to play an Australian barrister who, after copping a number of convict jokes, walks all over the British sensibility and wins the case . . . it was a superb victory.

The other show, *Happiness*, was the brainchild of beloved British comedy star Paul Whitehouse, who was so sweet in the audition that he wrote an episode around me. 'G'day I'm Bev, the Aussie traveller who comes to stay for a night and ends up staying months!' It was great to see how a British crew work on location and, more importantly, how they spend the catering budget. I must say, when the sticky date pudding made an appearance after lunch on the shoot, I was very pleased.

No sooner had I finished filming these two roles than Christmas was upon me. Christmas in a cold country is something quite unusual for me. Normally I have the whole catastrophe at my mum and dad's with my family, the traditional huge hot lunch followed by a sleep by the pool in heat that feels like it is melting the pavers. When the weather is a steady four degrees the pool doesn't sound like such an attractive offer.

The real highlight of the festive season in London is the lights on display in the streets of the West End. They are turned on in early December and for some reason make you want to spend any money you have.

After Superman flew away, I didn't have a partner to spend Christmas Day with. But I wasn't alone in that. Most Aussies in London will meet at someone's postage-stamp-sized flat and have what we call an 'orphans' Christmas. The main order of the day is to eat and drink to excess and then fall asleep in front of whatever heating apparatus is around. (So, except for the pool, it is all very similar!)

Boxing Day, in my opinion, should always be reserved for your best gay friends, in order to have a proper recovery with great wines, a feast and, well, basically the same as Christmas Day except you are certain to have a selection of extremely handsome men at the table. (Pull that cracker!)

That year I spent Boxing Day with Angus, my delicious flatmate 'baby Benny', Christopher from *Liquid News* and a few men who cannot be named because I can't actually remember them. River Café lemon tart is what I do remember and loads of disco naps interspersed with disco music.

The New Year kicked off and, with not much money to speak of, we were all back to work with what felt like more of the same-same. London is like that. One month I felt like I was really getting on top of things financially and then the next month I couldn't work out where it all went as I struggled to pay my tube fare. So I was off, yet again, touring around the country, with odd jobs coming in on radio and little bits of television to add to my *Liquid News* appearances.

Looking back I feel like there is loads of time missing in my memory but I am sure this is because my life during the London winter was unbearably repetitive. I worked, drank too much and then fell into a coma-like sleep before starting all over again. I was never much of an alcohol-loving girl before arriving in the UK but when you can't afford to get out of the city you tend to get out of your mind.

I had stayed reasonably clear of booze in my twenties because I was on television. I didn't want to be seen falling out of nightclubs every night of the week. I did have a few vinos but I never really got that stuck into it, plus I have quite low blood pressure, which means hangovers are even more ferocious, like walking around with an axe through the back of your head. In Britain I 'Let the Balloon Go' and inevitably found myself doing the walk of shame on a regular basis. It is a weird thing to brag about, but Aussies think that we are big drinkers (and we are), but the British drinking culture is in another league altogether. In the UK it is quite socially acceptable to have a hangover. I never really got used to it. I would wake up in the morning and think, Who do I have to apologise to today?

Let me give you a classic but not isolated example. I had met a Melbourne girl named Janine who was way too fabulous, on a trip home to Sydney, in fact she hurt my feelings she was so amazing. Janine was funny and so genetically gifted that every time we got ready to go out she would come into the loungeroom and I would end up thinking, What is the point going out when she looks like that and I look like . . . this?

Before I left for London at the end of my holiday she said to me, 'My brother lives in London and he is a spunk and hilarious, so I am going to demand that he takes you out for a drink.' I thought this was the best news ever.

I wasn't long back in the Capital (the name locals call London) when the brother sent me an email. (I'm going to call him 'Mr X' during this chapter to protect his privacy and to add to the dramatic effect.) The email went a bit like this . . .

> *Hi Funbags,* [my nickname from years ago when I worked as a receptionist for one of Sydney's top realtors – hi John]
> *My sister tells me that you are into 'overnight romance' which is something we may have in common. She also tells me that I need to take you out for a wine or two. So if you are up for it just let me know and we can make a plan.*
> *X*

Can you do me a favour and just read that email from Mr X again? How sexy is it? As I read it over and over and over again, I kept wondering what font I would use on our wedding invitations. I am mad for ITC Mona Lisa Solid and of course who is not partial to the casual lean of Handwriting Dakota . . . but enough of that, plans had to be made.

I emailed him back and he told me to pick a night and a location and we were on. I wanted him to think

I had a finger on the London pulse so, hoping to impress him, I took myself down to the St Martins Lane Hotel to see if there was any chance of us booking into the Light Bar.

London is very snobby when it comes to its hip hotel bars. Most of them require you to be a private member (for thousands of pounds a year) or be staying at the hotel to get in. I just knew the Light Bar would be the perfect location for our drink. In 2002, it was seriously chic, with funky lighting and private booths, full of the total 'it' crowd from London's art, film, pop and TV scenes.

Can you believe my luck when I struck a boy at the reception desk who was from Adelaide? He said to me, 'I used to watch you on TV when I was little [yes, thank you] and I love you,' so using my fame from yesteryear, he booked me in. I emailed Mr X to say, 'Let's just meet at the Light Bar 'cause it is easy' (being aloof can be so draining), and we were set.

Finally the night came and we were meeting at 6pm. Feeling like a million bucks, I stepped out in a chocolate and muted-pink figure-hugging Saba fine wool frock, teamed with a dreamy ox-blood Kenneth Cole heel. I could not have chosen a better position for our booth: it was private but still close enough to the action.

Arriving first, I ordered a glass of Australian sauvignon. Now, I have to ask you, why do groovy bars always serve wine in glasses so big that you could use them as a bucket to soak your smalls in? The glass was silly massive but I was so nervous that I necked its contents in no time. Just as I ordered a second tipple my date walked through the door. Oh, my giddy aunt, I knew it was him, tall and tanned and young and lovely (I think I started to drool), with a perfectly cut suit, a rocking haircut and really expensive shoes. Mmm, come to Mumma.

Conversation could not have gone more smoothly; it felt like we had known each other for years. He was so very charming that I didn't notice exactly how many buckets of wine I had consumed. When I went to the ladies' room I managed to use some of the hallway walls as a directional guide. Texting baby Benny with the letters P.N.E.H. (potential new ex-husband), I drew the phone closer, then further away, then closer again in order to focus. The little envelope flew away and I was back to a fresh bucket of pinot.

Mr X suggested we go out and have a bite to eat but I had a better idea. Why live in the West End and not utilise the proximity? I countered his suggestion with a garbled 'let'sgoto myplaceandIwill-cooksumpasta'. So we headed across the road to the supermarket where we were getting on so well that it felt like we had been a couple since the dawn of time. I was playing coy in herbs and spices and he was being fresh in produce. This was the best date in the history of dates.

We got home (baby Benny had made himself scarce) and I decided to show Mr X how I knew my way around the kitchen, obviously part of my 'subtle' campaign to show how stylish, funny and whiz-ish in the kitchen I can be.

The bacon, cream, onion and bit of seeded mustard trying to masquerade as carbonara never did rise to become quite the impressive culinary delight I had predicted. We had swapped to a cabernet by then and everything was going fine until the pasta reached the point of *al dente*.

Why I would attempt to remove the saucepan from the heat with no gloves or tea towel remains a mystery to me to this day. Halfway between the stove and the sink I realised what I had done, as the searing white pain started to shoot up my arms. Not wanting to cause a scene I simply put the pan into the sink and asked Mr X could he please turn on the cold water so I could remove my fingers from their prints.

The dish was actually a hit but I was in no mood for eating. My hands were aching as my fingers shrunk into petrol-dipped gypsy claws*. Despite this, I soon felt it was time for us to adjourn to the sitting room where we decided to call Mr X's sister.

* 'Petrol-dipped gypsy claws' is an expression I've been using since I met the Gypsy Kings years ago on tour in Noumea in the South Pacific. I asked them about their very strange nails and they told me that as kids they used to dip their fingers in petrol so the nail melts off, then they file and file the new nail, then dip again until it ends up looking like a claw so they can pick their guitars. Euh.

Janine was in great form and was so pleased we were out together.

I am not too sure of the time-frame after the call but I know it wasn't long before I felt the need to turn into Larry the Lunger and make my move. I leant forward to kiss Mr X but sadly miscalculated both the distance and his interest, resulting in me head-butting him in the teeth.

He got such a shock that he jumped up, made some sort of 'having to get up early' excuse and made his way to the front door. If you think my shame file should stop there, then read on and weep with me. The last thing I can remember that night was standing at the front door screaming at the disappearing Mr X, 'Come back, surely a pash is not going to hurt you.' I know. It's almost as hard to write down as it was to live through.

I woke up the next morning feeling very relaxed for those first few seconds of consciousness and then it happened . . . BOOM. Memory and pain hit me like a steam train. Oh my, has there been an act of terrorism in my head overnight? Quickly followed by No No. No. No. No. Noooooooooooo. I felt so very ill as I pulled myself from my bed to send an email to Mr X saying that I had no idea who that freaky girl was in my flat the previous night but rest assured she was gone forever.

He returned my message with the most lovely response, saying, 'It is not often I am lavished with the affections of a beautiful stranger' . . . all together, *aawww*.

I never heard from him again.

The remainder of that day was filled with a combination of fear and loathing mixed with vomiting and regret. I was feeling very sad and sorry.

At about 5pm my mobile rang and the incoming caller ID showed me that the producer from *Liquid News* was calling. If any guests dropped out of the show at the last minute I was always on standby to fill in. I loved it and enjoyed the extra money but that day I thought about not answering. I was way too unwell to go into the Beeb but I couldn't let it go. I pressed the answer button and let out a croaky hello.

‘Hi Julia, sorry to disturb you at home but I wanted you to hear it from us first. Christopher has been found dead in his flat . . .’

I didn’t hear the rest of the conversation. I just hung up the phone and wept.

3

The One

Hearing of Christopher's death shocked me to the core. It was so out of the blue. Even though outside work we had only been in the early stages of friendship – nights out in Soho quite a few times, he had come to a few of my shows and we'd spent that wonderful recent Boxing Day together – in my mind I didn't see our friendship ending. I expected to know Christopher forever. He was 34, funny, kind and I am sure destined for even greater success. I felt hollow and sad that he had died before we could get to know each other even better, like something precious had been lost.

The weeks following Christopher's death were very bizarre. He'd been a 'hard news' journalist for years and had managed to cross over into entertainment successfully, which is quite rare. I'm sure he was the envy of loads of journos who dreamed of escaping the thankless grind of daily news. With his sudden death he *became* the news. There was much speculation in the press and claims surfaced that he had died from an overdose of barbiturates. Despite no real evidence to support it, the question was asked – was it an accident or suicide?

To me and many others the whole notion that he had killed himself made no sense. In the short time I'd known him he was certainly no big-time party boy. I guess family and friends always find any suggestion of suicide impossible to believe but in Christopher's case I was sure suicide was wrong. He seemed to me very happy, very successful and even though he was hard on himself at times he was not a dark character subject to swinging highs and lows.

The day after he was found dead, a number of BBC presenters he'd worked with were asked to come in and say a few words on camera for a special dedication to his life. I was grateful to be asked, and to have a chance to honour Christopher and his memory. I had (thankfully) never done something like this before and I was emotional and found it hard to stay composed. Everyone I spoke to felt the same; they were in shock and not sure what to believe about his death.

Christopher's funeral was held at the Brompton Oratory in South Kensington, the second largest Catholic church in London after Westminster Cathedral. It was a beautiful and grand send-off for such an understated man. I had not realised that, like me, Christopher was a 'resting' Catholic. Considering how the Church feels about, as Christopher would say, 'homosexxxual/gays', the location was its own tribute.

The wake was held on the rooftop of Century, an extremely chic private club in the West End. Christopher's close friends, work friends and a few family members all gathered to celebrate knowing this lovely man. We managed to toast him with quite a few wines and we all agreed that there had to be another explanation. It is natural to search through your memories for any signs that had been missed but no one there that night believed Christopher had taken his own life.

It would take two months, but eventually the coroner's report revealed the truth: Christopher's death was from natural causes. The most distressing thing is that the speculative suicide reports of a person in the public eye generally appear as banner headlines with no regard for the family's feelings, but any evidence to the contrary is buried. You will find retractions months later, but you are lucky if they appear before page 17. In Christopher's case the coroner found that he died from meningoencephalitis, a medical condition that is a deadly combination of both meningitis and encephalitis that causes inflammation of the brain. Christopher had been unwell and battling an ear infection he had seen his doctors about. He had been treated for it, but tragically the medication exacerbated the brain swelling. As far as the public's perception of his cause of death, the report was too little, too late.

Without ever knowing it, Christopher had given me so much in my lonely and depressing early days of living in London. He didn't just give me a job, he put out his hand and pulled me into a spotlight that just kept getting brighter. I will never forget him for that. He was a gentleman on every level and I still miss him.

Without Christopher, *Liquid News* hobbled along with a number of different replacement hosts. For a while it seemed to lose all direction and spark while the network decided what they wanted to do with it. Being a guest on the show was nowhere near as much fun as it had been when Christopher was at the helm. Each 'try out' host was determined to bring their own style but hardly any of them had the gift for combining news journalism with witty entertainment and sharp topical comments. To be fair, it is hard to listen to a guest while the director talks through your earpiece about what or who was coming up next. The contenders were all so intent on doing the job well that none of them relaxed into the show. They didn't react to what was happening and respond accordingly to the banter. Time and time again I would deliver a funny line and instead of laughing, commenting and moving on, most of the new hosts would simply turn to the camera and reply with a distracted 'yes'. The fusion that Christopher had achieved with his guests was gone and so too was the magic.

But despite losing Christopher, some of his ideas stayed alive. One of the shows he'd had in production was called *Liquid Eurovision*, a live show presenting and commenting on the European institution that is the Eurovision Song Contest. For those of you who have never been exposed to its special brand of showbiz magic, this is an annual singing competition held among active member countries of the European Broadcasting Union. Perhaps its biggest achievement so far is bringing Abba to the world. Do I need to say more?

Each member country submits a song to be performed on live television and then casts votes for the other countries' songs to determine the most popular song in the competition. The contest has been on air every year since 1956 and it is one of the longest-running television programs in the world. It is also one of the most-watched non-sporting events in the world, with audience figures numbering anywhere between 100 million and 600 million internationally. It is tragic . . . but it is gold.

I was to co-host *Liquid Eurovision* and, frighteningly, the show was thrown together the day before it was due to air. We were broadcasting from the BBC studios in London even though the contest was in Estonia. Until then I admit I had only ever seen short snippets of Eurovision. So you can imagine my surprise when the whole thing kicked off and I flashed back to watching a talent quest heat on the centre stage outside the doughnut shop in the Imperial Centre in Gosford. I felt like I had televisual concussion and reacted accordingly, making fun of the whole spectacle every time the camera turned to me.

Okay, so this is where I have to admit to committing one of my greatest live-to-air faux pas (to date). It was my turn to commentate while Germany was on. I would have been fine except the German entrant was this rather sturdy, blonde, severe-looking woman, who reminded me of a nun who taught me in Year 8. However, unlike the nun, she was dressed in a particularly questionable head-to-toe leather ensemble and was singing like a Viking.

When it came time to give my thoughts on her performance I had a bit of a rant. It went a little like this: 'How awesome is this woman? She looks like the full fruit and nut bar in her "Your the voice, try and understand it" full-length leather trench coat and I could not be more delighted by her make-up and that she is still pushing the "I wear my sunglasses at night" statement from the late '80s. She looks like one of those ping-pong-mouth clowns at a carnival.'

My fellow commentators appeared quite disturbed and one of them said, 'Julia, she is blind.'

Oh – whoopsie!

Not convinced the BBC would ever employ me again after that, I was quite astounded when my agent called me with a very exciting offer. The Beeb were going to break *Liquid News* up into a few different nights and were wondering if I would be interested in co-hosting the Friday night show, which was going to be the round-up for the week. Did they even have to ask?

The new show was planned to start in September, which was perfect timing for me as I had committed to a few shows at my third Edinburgh Festival and was taking my first non-work holiday since I had arrived in the UK before I made my way to Scotland. (Angus and I really did work frightfully hard in Bellapais and you will just have to believe me that it was time for a holiday!)

Each year since I had moved to London, my best male friend, Juzzy, had come over to visit for a few weeks to work, rest and play before hitting the continent for a few more weeks. He'd finally head home to Australia needing a holiday. If you look up the expression 'finger on the pulse' you will more than likely find a picture of Juzzy. We met in 1988 when I was a GO (guest organiser) for Club Med on the French Pacific island of New Caledonia. He had come with a few friends and I was there waving a palm frond to welcome him. We bonded over bar beads, models and skinny-dipping and have had an extremely solid friendship ever since. Juzzy is a mobile party who always turns up with loads of funsters in tow.

During my first year away he came to my opening night in Edinburgh as a súrprise and stayed for a few extremely blurry days. The second year he threw a party at a very stylish restaurant-cum-private bar called '7' on Leicester Square that is closed now but still spoken of in legendary terms (both the place and the party). For this third year, after listening to my tales of woe about my ongoing negative financial situation and the ups and downs of life in London, Juz decided to scoop me up and take me to Italy and then to the South of France on holidays.

I didn't fight the idea. (I may often be blonde, but I am not stupid.) Not content with the usual touristy locations, we did some research and found one of the Mediterranean's hippest hotels on the volcanic Aeolian Island of Panarea, just north of Sicily.

We met up in Naples. Juzzy, who is the chairman of Sotheby's in Australia, arrived directly from some sort of Klimt conference in Zurich so was full of outlandish stories. I had come directly from my flat so my tales were not nearly as interesting. I was happy to sit back in a Naples bar with a wine or two and listen to Juz entertain me. The view of Pompeii made us both quite thirsty so the holiday sensation didn't take long to invade my blood. Before I knew it, it was time to wobble our way to the cruiser that was transporting us on the three-hour journey to Panarea.

Our hotel was carved into the hillside of the island, with an insanely exquisite view of the Med. Hot-pink bougainvillea splashed out against whitewashed buildings dwarfed by the cliffs rising above them. This is one of those locations you go to in your life and when you look back at the breathtaking photos you still cannot believe you were ever there.

Juzzy and I had adjoining rooms, which meant a shared balcony for the three Rs: reading, resting and rosé. We read to relax, sampled rosé 'cause it's rude not to, and rested up as much as possible during the daylight hours to prepare for the red-hot hotel open-terrace nightclub that attracted the most ravishing Europeans within a 100-kilometre radius.

The holiday is all rather blurry now (did I mention rosé?) but I did manage to get myself acquainted with a strapping young Roman dentist who lived in New York. He was so handsome I felt uncomfortable looking at him directly in the face for fear of turning to salt. Oddly, I remember *that* evening as if it were yesterday. It was one of those nights you look back on and wonder how you were not attacked or even killed.

I'd folded myself into a black Herve Leger classic strapless mini and pair of flat black crystal 'Jesu' slides for the night's festivities, so was feeling not too shabby when I accepted an offer to go out to the dentist's yacht. I told Juz I was going and he offered to come along as chaperone. That seemed silly to me, especially as I wanted to make some Italian enquiries into a bit of kissing on the lips, so he agreed to stay behind to make his own enquiries, telling me to make sure I was back in time for our transfer to the mainland at 8am. I had a few hours till then.

It wasn't until we were in the little motor boat heading out to the yacht that I realised just how many wines I had consumed. I started to feel more than a little bit dizzy. Stepping up onto the yacht I noticed there were already three other men on board. They were all very handsome but, nevertheless, now we were five. Not exactly what I had planned. I made some small talk and kept things light but I was feeling increasingly nervous and increasingly unwell. I wasn't feeling tipsy at this point, just sick. So sick, I had to ask to be shown the bathroom to have a ride on the big white china bus.

After I'd been in the bathroom for quite a while making the sorts of noises necessary when emptying the contents of your stomach over and over again, the dashing young man with whom I had made the journey knocked on the door, and asked if I would like to return to the island. What a splendid suggestion. I must have looked like a real stunner when I opened the door still wiping my face. I climbed back on deck into the fresh air and made my way gingerly down to the dinghy. I could hear the sniggers from the men on the deck – they were all smirking and talking in Italian so I couldn't understand what they were saying. I felt like some sort of failed stripper and wanted the earth (or ocean) to swallow me up.

The journey back to the quay was thankfully short, but halfway there the boat engine just cut out. My 'date' told me we had run out of petrol. Hmmm . . . surely it wasn't a line. Not to be dissuaded from getting back to my room and retaining some of my dignity, I picked up an oar and in the style of Zena not-quite Warrior Princess, the power rose up within me and I rowed us back into shore. Nowadays, my friends wonder why I don't really drink much. Let's face it, I have had my go at it!

Not surprisingly, I went back to my room alone. I couldn't find my key, so rather than disturb Juzzy, who I was sure was now fast asleep, I decided to sleep on our balcony. *Zzzzzzzzzzzz* . . . I woke up in daylight with my lips stuck to the cushion from an alarming amount of sleeping drunkard's dribble. I had no idea of the time when I knocked on our balcony door and was let in. To say my old friend was not impressed would have to be the understatement of the year.

It was much later than I thought and we had already missed our transfer. Juzzy was so concerned when I hadn't returned to my room he had raised the alarm. The last time he'd seen me I was heading off on a boat with a mysterious Roman, so he was imagining the worst possible scenarios and had called on the hotel staff to look for me. Can you bear it? I was so sick I couldn't deal with the many levels of cringe I was experiencing. Have you ever heard of the Hall of Mirrors? It is a metaphorical place where you can take a good long hard look at yourself. I needed to visit it for a week, but there was no time.

I let reception know I was alive and was touched by their relief. They immediately organised another boat (to get us out of their hotel) to take us to the mainland. We had quite a day of travelling ahead of us, and feeling as bad as I did, the only way I thought I could cope was to put on a tantalising, eco-chic, Tencel-denim singlet mini dress and red patent Gucci wedges for the trip. I then completed one of my longest ever walks of shame as I made my way from my room, through the foyer and down to the dock. I couldn't bear to look people in the eye so I had the whole bowed head thing happening, but at least in my delusional brain I thought I looked hot.

Hot was not at all what I felt after the boat ride back to Sicily. Thanks to my slumber on the balcony (sounds so much better than drunken interlude) we missed our cheap bus transfer for the three-hour journey to Palermo airport. Fabulous! There was nothing else we could do but to cough up for a taxi. I was still broke so Juzzy paid. Three hundred and fifty Euro later (AU$677) we arrived at Palermo airport about two minutes before take-off. By this stage my hangover had lifted but my feelings of disgrace hadn't. In fact they still haunt me, even to this day.

We flew from Sicily to Milan, changed planes then flew to Toulouse before driving for an hour and a half to a palace in Carcassonne. Some people might have made me suffer longer but I was lucky because Juzzy let me off the hook early in the trip. By the time we arrived safely in Toulouse I was totally forgiven. I don't know if I would have been so gracious if it had been the other way around . . . I might have sulked and acted righteous for a few days longer at least. All was back on track for a fabulous holiday, well, almost. Unfortunately our luggage didn't arrive at the same time we did.

A week in the South of France, residing in a friend's private mansion overlooking the Pyrenees with none of your belongings is nowhere near as relaxing as it sounds. Let's just say that after four days of rinsing my smalls and my now not-so-tantalising, eco-chic, Tencel-denim singlet mini dress I was over it. I had no moisturiser, no deodorant, no cossie, no nothing. I did manage to borrow a (wait for it) one-piece, highlighter-yellow fluorescent, low-legged swimsuit, complete with action back. Trust me, not very alluring. The only thing that kept me sane was being seen pool-side in my red Gucci heels. Thank goodness for small mercies.

When I finally got home to London I was thrilled to have a change of clothes and underwear that didn't smell like a cake of Palmolive. When the luggage finally turned up two weeks later it seemed like a massive anti-climax but the tracking information from the airline suggested the bags had an even better holiday than we did.

I wasn't home long before I was packing again, but this time it was because I was moving. In an attempt to escape a deranged flatmate, Benny and I had made a rush move into a fantastic flat in North London. The flat was part of a converted church and the windows in our bedrooms were the ornate stained-glass sides of the formerly reverent building. It was beautiful and had caught both our imaginations so we didn't think past the interior. We should have. The real estate agent who showed us the place called the location 'Highgate borders'. Highgate is a very sought-after area and has been home to many famous dignitaries and stars over the years. Karl Marx is buried there, which, for some, is reason alone for it to be feted.

The strange thing is, when I looked on a map, our 'church' was shown to be in Archway, a much rougher area and home to many council estates. Now I am not here to judge but let me put it this way, the local Archway site of interest is a landmark referred to as 'suicide bridge'.

You'd think by now (especially after the Roman dentist fiasco) I would have learned that just because something is gorgeous it doesn't mean it is perfect or right for me. Men . . . flats . . . same lesson. But I didn't learn the easy way, so Benny and I moved in haste and regretted at our leisure.

I wasn't there long before a friend and I were robbed of our mobile phones. My friend, TV's Carolyn Ashton, had come over to take me out. Carolyn got the nickname TVCA after an altercation years before with a laptop. (Carolyn is a high-energy fashion-guru television presenter who makes Heidi Klum look matronly!) As the story goes she was on her way to Paris for a show and was running so late that she was trying to blowdry her hair with two cheapy hairdryers. As each one overheated and turned off she used the other one. She ran out the door of her London flat not realising she had left both of them on . . . so when she returned four days later her laptop disk drive was melted to the floor. She got a fright when one of the hairdryers turned on, giving her the heads-up as to how the meltdown had happened.

She decided to ring the laptop manufacturer and tell them it had melted in the hope of getting a new one (leaving out the blowdrying detail). She was getting nowhere with them until she introduced herself as TV's Carolyn Ashton – suddenly the service got much better.

It got so much better in fact that every few days TV's Carolyn Ashton got a call from the company telling her where the computer was now. They could not work out the problem in London so the computer went to Germany. When they could not work out the problem there, it went off to Japan . . . they were all dumbstruck.

We laughed so hard thinking of the scientists and technicians looking at the computer thinking 'how is it so?', not realising in a million years that it was two renegade blowdryers from Woolies. Whoopsie. They replaced the laptop and Carolyn was known ever after as TVCA. So when TVCA and I were robbed of our mobile phones we chalked it up to karma!

Benny got into local trouble too. On his way to the bus stop, he was surrounded and pushed around by a group of very scary teenage youths (whom we'd seen gathering every afternoon at dusk like Alfred Hitchcock's *The Birds*). There was a constant feeling of menace about the place. God had obviously moved on when the church was deconsecrated. The final straw was when Benny and I witnessed a fight outside the flat one night that moved quickly from fists to sawn-off shotguns. That was it for us; we were on the move again.

Talk about going from the sublime (if you focused on the interior and ignored the crime) to the sensational! We found what could only be described as a three-bedroom 'pad' right on the ultimate posh shopping strip of Knightsbridge. The famed ultra-glamorous department store Harvey Nichols was our local milk bar and Harrods was our 7/11. We had suffered enough and now it was time for us to be stepping up. My new job on *Liquid News* meant I could lay out a whisper more in rent and Benny was a young director of a very impressive advertising agency so we felt like a couple of 'Yuppets'. Times certainly were a-changin'.

I had only spent two nights at the new palace when it was time for me to pack again and head up to my fourth Edinburgh Festival. Now I know I have mentioned the festival so many times already, but for comedians in the UK it really is our version of the end-of-year office party. It feels like you know everyone in town and the second you arrive there are about a thousand friends to party with. The work is only that little annoying bit that needs to be done before the non-stop jollification can start.

I had no idea as I arrived at Kings Cross Station, ready to take the familiar Flying Scotsman journey, that my world was about to be rocked in a profound way.

After four hours of travel I was greeted at the station by one of my dearest friends, Fraser, who is the PR guru of Scotland. We had met a few years before and had decided it was necessary to have time restrictions on our outings, as we both took turns at being the bad influence. Too much naughtiness.

'A traditional afternoon Scottish Gin Party is what you need, my dear,' Fraser said with a twinkle in his eye as soon as he saw me. I have since found out there is no such tradition nor party. It was just his way of getting me into Ricks, an ultra-funky yet laidback bar, so we could make ourselves available to a splash of post-lunch Bombay Sapphire in the form of their highly recommended 'Flirtinis'. (Like I needed much convincing.)

No sooner had we left Ricks than we were required at the Forth Floor bar in the newly opened Harvey Nichols store to sample a selection of French bubbles. The drinks were starting to rise like a spirit level in my eyes when Fraser suggested that we have a spot of tapas.

Since when does a couple of discs of spicy sausage and a few tiny squares of potato fill the tummy of a lady who is clearly on a party mission? Our next location was the Library Bar at the Guilded Balloon, one of the three major venues of the festival. By that stage we had retired from the good stuff and started necking Chateau Cardboard. I cannot even imagine how fascinating I thought I was by that stage, but before I could have an epiphany it was time to move off to meet some friends at the Assembly Room's Star Bar.

Seeing the look of alarm on the faces of my pals should have registered but by this point my eyes were all spirit and I was definitely unbalanced. They asked if I was okay even though they could clearly see that I was anything but. I shrugged an answer then ignored them as I spied this familiar-looking spunk in the corner.

I had met this guy a couple of times before through my buddies Crispin and Jules. I obviously still had enough brain cells left to remember that his name was Dan. He had that look that made me think, 'Oh my God, I must pash you at some point.' It just seemed silly not to make that night the point. Falling over chairs and no doubt dribbling through a smile, I transformed myself into Harry Suave and started to romance this dark-haired man. (Gosh, how tempting I must have been, the poor guy never stood a chance.) I was not so much playing 'hard to get', but 'hard to want'.

Apparently I told the same anecdote four times before Jules, Crispin and Dan suggested we should grab a coffee and something to eat. It was their very sweet way of getting me out of the venue before I really made a total goat of myself.

When I bumped into a number of people the next day they were all highly concerned about my health. Thinking this was quite strange, I asked one of them to elaborate and he said to me, 'Well Julia, you arrived at Assembly last night in the same state that most people leave the festival in.' Oh, and he kindly added . . . 'It was when you slid into the bar like Tom Cruise in *Risky Business* that most of the room decided to give you a wide berth.'

Why is there always one person willing to be the merchant of doom? I can't bear that. Our conversation was interrupted by my ringing mobile. It was Dan.

Dan: 'How are you feeling?'

Julia: 'Not too bad, all things considered.'

Dan: 'I was wondering if you'd like to have some dinner tonight after your show?'

Oh my stars, my show. My head felt like a smashed piñata and I had forgotten it was the opening night of my show.

Julia: 'That would be lovely, Dan.'

Dan: 'Great, I will come and collect you from the theatre.'

The show that night was a hit and the audience filed out buzzing. I love stand-up. It gives a performer the chance to speak from their truth, to become an opinionated, authoritative and at times almost ferocious voice of their generation, as long as it is funny. When I am on stage I say things and tell stories I would never reveal in normal company. Well, not often anyway.

I didn't realise Dan had been in the audience until the theatre was nearly empty. When it clicked that he'd just seen the show (and my performance the night before), I thought to myself, Well, this man has seen nearly all of the most full-on versions of me, so if he still wants to go out to dinner then there is hope!

Thankfully, Dan didn't disappear with the crowd so dinner was on. Wisely, I decided it was best to steer clear of any drinking and was on my best behaviour as we slipped into an effortless evening of conversation and laughter. I know I told you he is a spunk but I just don't think I had taken the time to notice how amazing he actually was. To be blunt, I was swept away by his fabulocity.

The next few days were like a montage from some daggy romantic comedy. We held hands and started to get to know each other as I managed to combine new love with doing a radio show alongside US comic sensation Greg Proops, then I added a few network meetings just to top off a very busy week. My head was quite literally spinning.

A few days later, I had to come back to earth, leave Dan and return to London to take promotional photos with the new *Liquid News* hosting team. They were all a little startled by the look on my face but perhaps it was the surface area of my pash rash. I remember the make-up artist describing it as a beard of scabs. That's nice, isn't it? Thirteen years of an all-girls Catholic private school education and in my mid-30s I am turning up to photo shoots with a pash rash . . . it was very 'Awstrayleean' of me.

The days while Dan was still up in Edinburgh seemed to crawl by. Why is it that when you meet a new paramour every second counts? The early difference with Dan and boyfriends from the past was that he wasn't hung up on some tragic macho day-counting crap before he called me. He wasn't over-the-top, but he wasn't afraid to let me know he liked me and missed me. It seemed that every time I would get that pathetic grin on my face while thinking of him, my phone would ring and it would be him wanting to tell me about something funny he had just seen, or just to say hello.

After an eight-hour drive he arrived in London and came straight to my place in Knightsbridge. Knowing he was coming I had decided that as soon as the intercom buzzer went off I would press play on Andrea Bocelli's 'Romanza', to try to make me sound real classy'n'that. In my opinion it never hurts to have those sexy Italian dulcet tones leaking through one's private home when a new love turns up at the door. The only problem was that unknown to me (who didn't check), the next disc to play was Phil Collins's 'No Jacket Required'. It didn't take long for Dan to realise I was nowhere near as cultured as I had pretended . . . D'oh. But he stayed around regardless.

I don't recall having the 'I am going to marry this man' feeling that night, but it has only ever been loving, easygoing and glorious from that day to this. Dan had just settled on the purchase of a flat the day he came back, so the next day he asked me if I would like to come with him to collect the keys and have a look around.

He picked me up in his dashing retro convertible muted-blue BMW and we sped off up a road that seemed very familiar to me. Can you believe that Dan's new flat was ONE STREET away from the church Benny and I had just moved out of? The difference was that Dan's flat was actually in Highgate itself, not in scary Archway. That is yet another really frustrating thing about London, just one street can be the difference between putting on the Ritz and needing a knife.

The day Benny and I left Archway we did a celebratory 'Ding dong the witch is dead' dance and agreed we would never ever return to the immediate area. Just to remind you, that dance had been executed a full week before. I shook my head in disbelief as Dan pointed out the features of the suburb. 'Really? Karl Marx, you say, how interesting.' There was no way I was letting a pact with my flatmate spoil the potential of this new relationship. I might be silly, but I'm not that stupid.

Actually, I am.

When I'm in the early stages of a relationship I turn into the very best version of myself. Helpful, fun, nothing is a problem and I'm always in great clothes with shaven legs so soft they could be mistaken for new-baby skin. It's only after a while that the cottontails come out and all bets are off.

We were still months away from the dreaded cottontails but things with Dan just continued to get better and better. Usually when I'm dating, it is only a few months into the fling before I start to see qualities I really don't like. I ignore them for the next couple of months, then I spend a month telling all my friends how I am going to have to end it, then another month actually pulling down the guillotine. This relationship was different. It was effortless. We just clicked and the clicking didn't show any signs of slowing down.

A big test would be the impending arrival of my parents. The thing about having your parents on the other side of the world is that when they finally come to stay, they stay for SEVEN weeks. Very relaxing, especially when you're still in the flush of new, big love. I'm sure Mum and Dad were equally as happy to see me but also equally perturbed by seven weeks of being under 'my roof'. My mum and dad like to sleep in when they're on holidays so they don't get up until at least 6am. Even with the lie-in these aren't exactly the same hours kept by their comedian daughter.

You can tell a lot about a man by how he behaves around your parents. Dan never displayed that 'false, nervous, polite guy' like so many men do. He was just himself and managed to allay what I knew was my parents' greatest fear: that I would fall for an English man and stay in the UK forever. Thank God Dan was Welsh, so they were okay – with interests in common, like me, everybody was happy.

It was great that my parents spent some time with Dan and got to know him very early in our relationship. I had started to tour Britain as Bob Down's support act, so I wasn't around as much as I had hoped, but Dan was fabulous about spending time with what I call 'Club Morris'.

When Mum and Dad headed home they knew I was completely smitten. I'd hooked up with Dan in August 2002 and by December we were going strong with no hint of cold feet from either of us. My usual patterns of relationship behaviour had been relegated to memory and despite the inevitable appearance of cottontails he was still treating me like I was one hot mama. Deciding to go on our first big trip away together, we chose sunshine over snow to celebrate Christmas in Jamaica. We didn't need to witness the female black Santa arriving by boat on Christmas morning to know we were falling in love, but by New Year's Eve in New York City, we were sure.

The year 2002 had been an absolute rollercoaster of emotion for me. After struggling to make a living and a name for myself in a new place, professionally things were gaining momentum. I'd embarrassed myself more times than I'd care to admit (so I won't) and I had learned to stand on my own two feet and be happy with who I was and the life I was making. I had made some wonderful new friends and strengthened old friendships. I lost someone I had come to care for, and perhaps that taught me to cherish those around me more. And then, when I least expected it, I lost my heart to a man who was secure enough in himself to love me back. I didn't know what 2003 would bring but I was looking forward to finding out, especially now that Dan was coming with me on the ride. Mmmm, kismet!

4

Suck that Lime, Mr Shaman

Without wanting to sound smug, I was a 30-something expat Aussie woman living the good life. As Charity Hope Valentine says so beautifully in *Sweet Charity*, that fickle finger of fate was pointing all the components of my life the right way. Work, home, relationship, family, wardrobe, even my finances, were all starting to be fabulous. Oh Happy Day.

Many years before, I had seen an elderly shaman in Singapore. He sliced a 'spiritual' lime in my honour (and that is not a euphemism), then told me that very rarely do the three sides of your *liiiife* triangle all go smoothly at the same time. Experience had taught me this already so it was no surprise. The other wisdom he passed on, which was more surprising and I remember it just as clearly, was: 'That will be a hundred spiritual US dollars, thank you.'

Well, the start of 2003 saw me having the time of my life, proving that shaman wrong, as the three sides (which, by the way, are love, work and health) were going way too well. Dan was a heavenly boyfriend, *Liquid News* was rating nicely thank you very much and I was feeling slim and magnificent. Suck that lime, Mr Shaman!

For the first time since I arrived in the UK my homesickness had all but disappeared. I would still have the occasional twinge, but the gut-wrenching sorrow I'd experienced three years earlier was only a distant memory. I was now half of a couple, which helped me feel more settled, but the fact that I was making headway in my career was also a huge factor. Even though *Liquid News* was only a six-month contract, it had opened so many other doors that my gig diary was full.

There were not as many perks working for the BBC news department as there usually are in commercial TV. I still had to get the tube to and from the studio each show day and I had to provide my own clothes. That meant doing any extra work I could get to keep up with the shopping necessary to be a stylishly dressed TV host.

A big part of my extra weekly income came from doing 'warm-ups'. A warm-up artist is the person in a television studio who entertains the crowd before filming starts and during the recording breaks. It's actually a vital role – the idea is to keep the audience's energy up and keep them listening and laughing during the long recording session, usually from about 6.30pm to 10pm. If you are going to see a comedy filmed in a television studio, the warm-up artist can be the difference between being part of an engaged and entertained audience or a participant in a hostage situation. Trust me when I say it can be a very fine line.

Warm-up gigs are quite highly prized by comics in the UK as they are not only a stepping stone right into the laps of the production companies, but can earn you the same amount of money working in a nice comfortable studio for a night as two or three nights in some smoky stand-up club at the other end of the country. Once I was in the loop, all sorts of comedy warm-ups started coming my way.

The first few shows I worked on felt quite surreal. While I was happy to take home such a nice fee for an evening's work, half the time I was warming up for the types of shows I had starred in back home. At times I couldn't help feeling I had taken a backward step and I would feel jealous, frustrated and a bit useless in what I would call these brief dark moments in my 'performing monkey' role.

Though we all love getting the gig, warm-ups can be a thankless task for comedians. Often you are only just getting on a roll and starting to pull the audience along when you have to stop mid-sentence because the cast and crew are ready to shoot. It's an awfully big job to harness an entire studio audience's attention when there is so much to look at around you. Even the movement of a light or the winding up of a cable can become interesting to the crowd and it hurts to be upstaged by a ladder. Not getting the chance to deliver the punchline at the end of a story can be crushing to a comic's ego (or is it just me?), but getting instructions from the 'stars' can be a whole lot worse.

One night-time show 'star', who had become better known for his acting rather than his long-since-faded days as a comic, asked me not to do any funny material before he came on. (He did say please.) That meant ten minutes of me talking without one joke and, let's face it, safety instructions can only be stretched so far! He also requested that I remain on the studio floor the whole time and not use any of the steps leading up onto his set, so I didn't upstage his entrance. Then, at the end of the show, he would ask me in front of the audience which bits I thought were the funniest. I was always tempted to say 'me', but never did.

At another warm-up gig, a male member of a sitcom cast, who were touted as the 'British Friends', would make fun of me every time I stepped out to entertain the audience during the filming breaks. He'd pull faces behind me as I spoke and pretend to pull down his pants to 'give it to me'. At first I couldn't work out why the crowd were laughing in some really strange places.

I suppose his behaviour was slightly better than that of some comic actors, who refused to acknowledge I was even there. Dealing with these rampant egos certainly made me think back through my own television years, wondering if I had ever disrespected another performer in the same way . . . but it's just not the 'Awstrayleean' way, so I am quite sure I didn't.

Most of the warm-ups went well (the one where I couldn't tell jokes was not my finest performance but what could I do?). Then I scored a gig that brought me face-to-face with one of my idols, a woman who had made me laugh so hard for so long. I was over the moon with excitement that I had landed the warm-up job for series six of her long-running sitcom, and slightly nervous too. Dan has a theory that you should never meet your idols because the meeting often fails on two levels. Firstly, they often don't live up to the 'God-like' creation you've built them up to be; and, secondly, because they are your idol and you are going to get so nervous you won't act as naturally or as sanely as you normally do, you then spend the rest of your life thinking, 'If only I had . . .'

When I arrived at the studio for the first night as my idol's warm-up, she and the other cast members greeted me and asked me to join them in the make-up room for a little splash of bubbly in a plastic cup to toast the success of the show. I instantly felt part of the team and was very appreciative at how friendly they all were. Someone told me they'd never had a warm-up artist before, but after making five series they were looking forward to something different. Although they were all busy with make-up and last-minute script changes, each cast member made me feel like I was a part of their family.

That night went so very well. Some friends visiting from home were in the audience so it felt like a special occasion, actually, special is an understatement. There are just some nights in a comedian's performing life when the planets seem to align and the audience loves you so much that they won't stop laughing long enough for you to get on with the next bit.

The planets were obviously in a complete, unwavering, army-issue straight line of alignment for me that night because the audience were screaming with delight and even stayed for 10 minutes after recording had finished to hear the end of one of my anecdotes. It was amazing. In the green room afterwards (the green rooms at the BBC are usually an old boardroom where the cast, crew and friends gather after the show to have a drink, a cold spring roll and a debrief) I did not have a moment to even speak to anyone because so many compliments were hurtling at me. My head was spinning; I was feeling soooooo sensational.

Two days later the producer called me at home . . .

Julia: 'I know why you are calling me!'

Producer: 'Really?'

Julia: 'How funny was I on Friday night?'

Producer: 'Yes, perhaps a little too funny.'

Julia: 'Are you ringing to tell me you've written a role for me in the show?'

Producer: 'Not exactly. Look, Julia. I am calling to let you know that we're going to have to let you go.'

Julia: 'Let me go where?'

Producer: 'Let you go. Finish your contract. We've decided not to have a warm-up artist for the rest of the series.'

I got such a shock that I went from cocky to crumpled in a split second. I was so ashamed of my bragging that I started crying. Not just crying, but that sob-speaking you do while gasping for a breath after each word.

Julia: 'What-(*sob*) did-(*sob*) I-(*sob*) do-(*sob*) wrong-(*sob*)? I-(*sob*) need-(*sob*) to-(*sob*) know-(*sob*) so-(*sob*) I-(*sob*) don't-(*sob*) do-(*sob*) it-(*sob*) a-(*sob*) gain-(*soooooobbbbb*).'

Producer: 'Look, it has nothing to do with you as such. XXX just thought that you stole all the laughs out of the room and there were none left for the script.'

Julia: 'What?' (*Sniff*)

Producer: 'But, we will pay you out for the entire series so you won't lose any money.'

Julia: 'Oh, okay.' (All of a sudden my crying seemed to calm right down.) 'Well, thank you.'

And that was that. I was sacked for being too funny. Is the whole world on drugs? How can a comedian be sacked for being too funny? I understand it can feel threatening when someone new comes onto the scene but this woman was an established legend. I was absolutely no danger to her at all. I couldn't believe it and from that moment I swore I would always embrace new talent and not try to block them . . . it just screams bad karma to stand in someone's way. As far as I am concerned that woman has watched *All About Eve* too many times.

I managed to get a whisper of payback when I went up to do my fifth Edinburgh festival later that year. I put a quote on my poster saying, 'She stole all of the laughs out of the room' and attributed it to my ex-idol. But the ultimate revenge came when I did some warm-ups for *The Kumars at No. 42*. Everyone involved in that show is seriously funny; they're all hugely talented performers/writers who are also generous spirits (I was learning the hard way that this was not a combination you find very often in my industry).

In a delicious twist of fate my (did I say now-former?) idol was the special guest on the show while I was involved. At the finish of filming, the magnificent Sanjeev Bhaskar came up to me, took my hand and made such a fuss of thanking me in front of the audience. Not knowing our history, he placed me directly in front of my former idol and blocked her from view. I took my bow then made my way to the side of the stage trying not to smile too widely. The taste of the humble pie I had been eating for so long was replaced by something much, much sweeter.

(I must make special mention of Catherine Tate here. She is *not* the nameless woman I have referred to above. Catherine is a goddess on about as many levels as you can think of. I was lucky enough to work on series one and two of her multi-award-winning BBC Two sketch show and I laughed through every magnificent minute of it.)

The 2003 Edinburgh Festival was also significant for another reason. I found out I was pregnant on the opening night of my show 'Will You Kids Get Out of That Pool Please' (I found out before the gig, not on stage, just in case you were wondering). The show was a photographic-slide, stand-up homage celebrating growing up in Australia. Weird that I was working on this and fell pregnant at the same time. It was like my subconscious was ready before me and my body caught up. Oh . . . and Dan was there as well, obviously. Dan and I had been together exactly a year and even though the first anniversary tradition is to give paper, we couldn't have been more excited at the thought of having a baby instead.

Those three sides of the triangle were positively humming. But what did that shaman say again? On stage I was so self-conscious of my early baby stomach sticking out that I used some of my *Liquid News* wages to shout myself an original Pucci spring print shift dress. It was perfect but halfway through the festival it somehow managed to find its way into the dryer and became a not-so-perfect top. Grrr.

Being pregnant meant my usual full-on Edinburgh experience was slightly different. Remember how the previous year I had delighted Dan with my Harry Suave alcohol-fuelled antics? Well, there was no sign of Harry this year. But we still caught up with lots of friends, ate far too much and adopted the usual comic/ vampire hours mixing business with pleasure.

After about three and a half weeks of the festival, a few days before it was due to close, the Scottish GP I was seeing suggested I might like to go for an early scan. Dan and I were quite casual about it. Great, a photo opportunity! We laughed and joked the whole time, never imagining anything could go wrong. We were still laughing when they told us the pregnancy was ectopic (in my tube). We didn't quite grasp what that meant at first. As soon as it sunk in we both stopped laughing very quickly. I don't really remember how I felt. Sad . . . scared. I had only a few minutes to digest the news when a surgeon suddenly appeared to introduce himself and check if I had eaten anything that morning. What the . . . ? He explained in that very precise surgeon way that I had to have emergency surgery. Not only was I not going to have this baby, it turned out that if we didn't hurry there was a chance that Dan would not have a partner. He finished his speech with 'please get into a gown'.

Ignoring the doctor's serious tone and Dan's worried expression, I made it known that this all seemed a bit sudden. I tried to explain that I still had two shows to go and I needed to clean the festival flat we'd rented. Once this was all done, and only then, would I be ready. I think I was still giving the surgeon my show-time schedule as the anaesthetist put on my mask and sent me out for the count.

Have you ever had morphine? When I woke up I was 'on the juice' and missing a fallopian tube. Dan said that every time I woke from my morphine cloud, I fired instructions on how to clean the flat until I faded out again. How insane is that? I had just lost a baby and I was obsessing about cleaning! 'That Jif under the sink I bought, make sure you *shevshuves-summ ksoiidfwiizzzzzz* . . .' and 'make sure the grout in *sk fowoe alkds ff azzzzzzzzzzzzzzz* . . .'

I was not in a good way and had to stay in hospital for seven days. Dan spent every one of those days and most of the nights at my bedside, making sure I had everything I needed and trying to cheer me up. The hospital was pure luxury, which is not usually the case in the UK medical system, but I was in a brand-new teaching hospital and had my own room. At any other time I might have been impressed but it all seemed so strange. I hadn't known I was pregnant long but the thought of becoming a mother had planted itself in my mind so I had to deal with the loss. With Dan around it was impossible for me to stay sad all the time though, especially when he went to the student shop and bought himself a stethoscope so he could listen to my heart. The nurses started to call him Dr Love!

When I was discharged Dan drove me back to London. We did have a bit of trouble on the *slooow* 12-hour drive home. We were listening to a BBC radio sketch show starring Mitchell and Webb and they were talking about opening a dry-cleaners and using a pun to name the shop. They decided to call the shop 'Touching Cloth' and the more they said 'touching cloth' the more Dan and I became hysterical with laughter. We were in such fits that I started to worry I was going to burst the 14 staples holding my abdomen together.

We had to pull the car onto the side of the freeway to regain some composure. I was aching by that stage and Dan's face was damp from floods of laughter tears. How my staples didn't burst and shoot across the freeway and kill someone is still beyond me. (I ended up doing studio warm-ups for Mitchell and Webb a few years later and I told them about how they nearly killed me – they loved it.)

Many couples have to cope with losing a baby, whether through a miscarriage or ectopic pregnancy. I had no idea how common this actually is – I found out that apparently one in every 100 pregnancies turn out to be ectopic and around 20 to 25 per cent of pregnancies end in miscarriage. It doesn't seem to be something many people talk about, but it was important for me to know that others had experienced what I had. But, being me, I don't ever linger on the sad stuff too long and if I did, Dan would pull me out of any hole, even though he was grieving too. The whole experience made me even more aware of how wonderful he was. This total Welsh spunk was definitely a keeper!

Being bedridden for the best part of five weeks while I recovered meant a huge loss in wages, but I had officially moved in with Dan before Edinburgh and we made the best of it. (I say 'officially' because we had already spent so much time together that I'm sure Benny felt abandoned long before I moved all my things to Dan's place.)

As soon as I was feeling up to it, Dan took me on a drive to one of his favourite lookouts above the historic settlement of Abersychan, overlooking the south Welsh valleys. I wasn't expecting it, but there, on bended knee (in a bit of sheep poo actually), Dan asked me to be his wedded wife. (All together . . . *awww*). And of course I said yes, before pointing out the sheep poo.

So, as a newly anointed and sufficiently recuperated fiancée, it was time to get back to work. My first show was with the supremely talented Stephen Fry, on his comedy-panel-game-quiz show called *QI*. The main idea of the show was not to answer the questions correctly but to come up with the most interesting or funny explanation. My brain was not quite back on deck but I managed the best I could in such illustrious, super-witty company as Alan Davis and Rich Hall. (I think my main contribution was cackling at anything the boys had to say, thus cementing the already deeply ingrained belief out there that women aren't really funny . . . *Grrr.*)

It seemed like the minute I got out of bed and went back to work that I got a call to do my show in Paris. With all the English-speaking ex-pats over there the belief was that ample numbers existed to manage a 'full house'. Many of my stand-up contemporaries have raved to me about how enjoyable the Paris experience is, so I was fairly keen to go – but a trip I had made there in early 2001 made me uncharacteristically tentative.

Back then, one of my closest friends, Flic, called to tell me she was going to Paris to catch up with her cousins for five days and wanted to know if by any chance I could make my way across the Channel so we could meet up.

Flic and I had met more than twelve years before at an outback picnic race meeting in Louth (about 830 kilometres north-west of Sydney). Someone pointed her out to me and said, 'Be careful of that one, she's wild.' Within the hour we became instant besties. Since then we've had many reunions all over Australia in places like Bourke, Dubbo, Melbourne, Sydney, Perth, Port Hedland, Darwin and even Broome, where she now lives.

I cannot emphasise enough how low my bank balance was at the time but there was no way I was not making an hour-long flight to Paris to see her when she had flown all the way from Broome. The husband of one of my London mates offered to sort out the trip for me, as he'd been to France quite a few times. I was surprised because he is normally a bit grumpy and I didn't think he listened when I whinged about my lack of money and latest dramas. Booking me on one of those budget airlines, he said, 'You don't need to buy an expensive ticket that flies straight into Charles de Gaulle Airport when the cheapy airlines land nearby.' So, thanks to him, I was heading off from London to St Etienne. I had £200 to my name but I wasn't worried. Maybe the fact that I took off smelling the underarm hair of the passengers squeezed in either side of me should have warned me that things were not going to be as easy as I thought.

I was sooooo excited about touching down in the land of garlic that I didn't realise straightaway that I was nowhere near Paris. Eventually I discovered I was in fact about 400 kilometres to the south of the capital. But it got worse. The only way to get to Paris from this 'nearby' airport was to cough up £160 (AU$400) for a ONE-WAY train ticket. I felt sick. Luckily I had already paid for my hotel but it meant I would only have £40 spending money for my five days in the City of Light. (And, of course, I had no idea how the hell I was going to get back to St Etienne for my flight home.)

I had no choice but to jump on the train (I'd worry about getting back later), and seeing Flic immediately made the journey worthwhile. She is the sort of seasoned travelling pioneer/adventurer who would have loved the challenge of my recent obstacles but I was so ashamed not to have any money that I kept my troubles to myself.

It turned out Paris has loads of free things to do and see that the only real outlay I had in the daytime was getting around on the Metro. Every morning I was extremely thankful for the breakfast included in my room tariff. I managed to back-in the croissant truck before each day's escapades then I would make various excuses about how I wasn't hungry whenever we stopped for lunch or dinner. (Have you ever been fainty-starving and watched someone at the next table lick a dripping shank of osso bucco with a duck-fat-fried fry? It makes you even more woozy.) At the end of each night I would pretend to head to bed and then I'd double back to the Maccas at the Bastille and dump a few coins on the counter for Le Big Mac. It really is amazing what you can live on.

Flic and I laughed all the way up the Eiffel Tower, through the Louvre and under the Arc de Triomphe. The days flew by and suddenly it was our last morning. I hadn't worked out a plan to get back to St Etienne so

I decided I had no choice but to ask Flic for advice. I was mortified to have to come clean about my financial woes. Why is it we feel such humiliation in front of the very people who would never judge us in a million years? She was upset I hadn't told her before and marched me straight to the Gare-de-Lyon (the main train station), handed over her credit card and paid for my return ticket to St Etienne. (More like Saint Flic, the Patron Saint of moronic friends.)

It was horrible saying goodbye but I daydreamed about the awesome time we'd had together for nearly the whole train trip, so it went quickly. I was brought back to reality when the conductor asked me for my ticket. Now although I took French for my School Certificate, *je ne suis pas fluent en Français.* The train conductor's English was as good as my French so we muddled through in a crazy mixed-up Franglais.

As I understood it, he said the train would not be going as far as St Etienne due to track travels (?) and so I was to get off at the next stop. Cool. I asked him if we were near the 'Avion' as I had to get on a plane (I used my hand to simulate 'take-off' as I said the word plane). He gave me the thumbs-up, so I was relieved.

The 'next stop' was the end of the train line. I looked around, dumbstruck. I was in the middle of a sheep paddock on a road to nowhere, with no phone, no money and if I missed the cheapy-no-refunds flight, no way of getting back to London. I thought it best to sit on my suitcase in the middle of the dirt road next to the track and cry. I cried and cried and cried, for ages. I watched the time ticking away on my watch, knowing my flight was due to take off in 1 hour, then 55 minutes, 50 minutes, 45 minutes, 30 minutes. I didn't know what to do and I'd never felt so useless.

In the distance, on top of the hill, I could see a tiny little dust cloud forming. The tiny little dust cloud got bigger and I stopped my sobbing. It was a little car driving towards me. The car came closer and closer until I could make out it was a tiny little Gendarme (policeman). It was like a scene from a Coen brothers' movie and far too surreal to be true. He stopped when he reached me and got out of the car speaking some very quick French. I just sat on my suitcase and started crying again, saying between sobs something along the lines of:

'Je besion faire allez le Aeroport pour prende Avion pour Londres, et jais pas de largent et par idee en generale. C'est possible vous avez un answer?'

This roughly translates to:

'Need I to be, to go airport for onto get plane London for and money I have no and no idea in general, you have one answer?'

Not surprisingly he looked a little confused but, sizing up the situation, he hand-gestured to his police car like he was a model on *The Price is Right*. I stopped crying and did what he signed me to do. He then proceeded to drive me to the St Etienne airport. He was my saviour. When I realised where we were heading I went slightly over the top with my *mercis* and they escalated to almost manic levels when we reached the airport.

I caught the plane in the nick of time. When I arrived safely back at Stanstead Airport I did have to ask someone at the ticket counter for money to get the train home, but that was nothing in the general scheme of shameful things I had already experienced.

So the thought of returning to Paris with more than just £40 was genuinely exciting. I decided to organise my own flights this time . . . just to be sure.

The venue for my Paris shows was the famed underground music club 'La Java', in the grungy yet artistic suburb of Belleville. The iconic French singer Edith Piaf had grown up in Belleville and made her singing debut at this club, which became such a favourite with her that whenever she performed in Paris she returned there at the end of each night to sing one final set before heading to bed.

For a girl from Gosford to be following in Edith Piaf's footsteps was amazing. I felt so honoured that this big emu was treading the same boards as 'the little sparrow'. And from the first night it was just the best. There were loads of Aussies in the audience along with many of what I call 'retired' Aussies. You know the sort of Australians who move overseas and become ashamed of where they come from, so somehow manage to lose the accent they've had for the best part of 25 years and replace it with a mangled variation of what they think the typical Parisian sounds like? I think the technical term for them is 'cockheads'.

One such 'former' Aussie came to speak to me after the show. I thought he was Basque (what I know as Gypsy French) judging from his accent but when I asked him about his origins he told me he was from Dapto, just south of Sydney. I passed him a drink and he patronisingly said, '*Merci*, that means thank you in French.' I replied, '*Bien sur, tu parle ou tu pete*?' Which loosely translates as, 'Are you speaking French or are you farting out of the front of your head?' He told me he had only been in Paris for two months and so had not picked up many local expressions as yet . . . (*tête de coq*).

Despite the cockheads, the shows went off like a backpacker's Christmas Day on Bondi Beach and not long after I was on the Eurostar, the super-glamour fast train, on my way back to my fiancé in London. He had a superb pressie waiting for me when I arrived home: a noble title.

Before I left for Paris, Dan and I had spent the most glorious three weeks with the supremo Australian TV writer Michael Idato, who was in Britain for his yearly visit to interview some of the biggest British TV stars. An old friend from my *Full Frontal* days, it was Michael who got away with putting me on the cover of the *Telegraph*'s TV magazine dressed as Nikki from *The Young and the Restless*. The man was without shame.

As a passing joke over an insanely tender Argentinean steak, Michael said to me, 'You know you cannot possibly return to Australia without a title.' He told us about websites where you can pay for one. It turns out that some members of the aristocracy have run out of family money so all they have left are the family estates. They managed to find a loophole in the law saying you only need to own a square inch of titled land to enable you to legally use a title and so they started selling it all off. I guess the main advantage is that no one comes to claim the land, they just use the title. (Although I did have a grand vision of going to the estate and planting a little cocktail flag with 'Lady J-Mo' written on it for my little square inch!)

Dan and I thought the whole idea was the best news ever . . . so I was delighted to arrive back home from Paris to find out I had become a Lady. Once we registered the paperwork with the Department of Nomenclature I officially became Lady Julia Morris on my driver's licence, passport and all of my banking documents. I am a Lady I am!

I have met countless British people who find the whole business of buying a title on the internet just appalling, but I think it really demystifies the British aristocracy and saves me from having to go through buying it from the government like so many others have done for centuries . . . but I guess not everyone feels that way. Oh well.

I don't know whether my title had anything to do with it, but more and more interesting work was coming my way. One very different booking was on the London Eye (the big, single-strut, don't-dare-call-it-a-ferris-wheel, overlooking the Thames). It was the site of a big charity event to help aid Fairtrade.

Every 'pod' of the Eye had different types of entertainment and it was the luck of the draw who you ended up with.

Some people were fortunate enough to do a revolution of the wheel listening to the acoustic charms of Blur frontman Damon Albarn; others were exposed to some poetry readings, mini plays and jugglers. Ten lucky ducks were thrust into a pod for the stand-up stylings of not just me but the very funny Gordon Southern. Gordon and I were quite surprised at how much it hurt to be upstaged by a view, but we both took it in our stride.

I had learned many lessons while working in Australian TV. During my twenties I thought I should be easygoing and show my enthusiasm so I said yes to every bit of media coverage on offer and every TV show that asked for me. It was devastating to then be told I was 'overexposed'.

A lesson I was learning in the UK was to ensure I was always 'match fit'. With stand-up, when you're doing well it's easy to become complacent about live work and yet if you let this slide you definitely lose your 'edge'. When you start to get a bit of financial security you have the luxury of choosing the work you want to do rather than the work you have to do to survive. This last one is where I often come unstuck.

During much of my time in London I had been forced to choose projects according to the dire state of my bank account. Though I had been lucky and scored some great work there was still the occasional career glitch. I was very proud of my sixth Edinburgh Festival show, which was the lead in a dramatic play called 'Hunting Diana', but maybe not so proud of the show called *Men in Frocks*. I took part in projects I might have turned down if I had the money to eat regularly. But a girl's got to eat.

As the great screenwriter William Goldman once said, 'Nobody knows anything.' He is so right. There will always be ample opinions on what makes a hit but it is virtually impossible to know what a show is going to be like before it's made. A massive blockbuster with an endless budget and a star-studded cast can just as easily turn out to be a turkey (think Kevin Costner's *Waterworld*), while a little indie project with a cast of unknowns can turn out to be the highest grossing picture of the year (have you seen *My Big Fat Greek Wedding* yet?).

Okay, so maybe the title *Men in Frocks* was a bit of a giveaway and I should have known better, but I harboured high hopes it was going to be one of those weird cult TV hits that comes up every now and then. The idea was to find six men who think that being a woman is easy, so easy they think they could make better women than their wives and girlfriends. If you try to imagine *It's a Knockout* meets *Transamerica* then you are, disturbingly, not even halfway there.

I took the gig and it was an . . . *experience*. Some of the contestants were very macho, so looked really wrong in dresses and high heels, but there were one or two who took to it a bit too easily . . . in a weirdy way. One in particular became quite bitchy and always left after filming with his make-up still on. He even went out and bought his own pair of heels. Mmm, can't blame him for that. Who doesn't love a good heel?

Anyway, if you are lucky enough to see the series I'm sure you'd think my favourite part was the grand final opening number, when I got to sing 'Man, I Feel Like a Woman' surrounded by all four finalists in black PVC-Shania-Twain 'skins'. You'd be wrong. That was nothing compared to the look on my face when they revealed the grand final winner's prize.

Through the previous five episodes, when it came time to mention the prize, we just used the words 'this new car' and the producers explained the footage was to be dropped in later. Well, as a concept, 'this new car' was technically correct, the car was new . . . to the winner.

It turns out that the show ran out of money halfway through production, so after a series of humiliating tasks like waxing, plucking, modelling gowns and cake decorating, the winner was presented with a light-blue 17-year-old bomb with no roof. Not convertible – no-roof, no actual roof. I think it even had rust marks. The winner looked more shocked than I did (well, they had to drive it!) and the crew started to laugh even before the curtain came down. Facing the very angry contestants after the show was one of the more horrible things I have ever had to do in the name of 'showbiz'.

I was hopeful that my days of bad career decisions were over. Without wanting to sound all Oprah-like, I had settled into my skin and both professionally and personally I was in a great place. And though that shaman had insisted all three elements of your life couldn't function well at the same time, I was determined to prove him wrong. Surely after my ectopic pregnancy nothing worse could happen . . .

No Place Like Home

Can you believe that in one year I had become a Lady and a fiancée? I don't know which my mother was more excited about. As time passed, though, the actual ceremony part of getting married kept being pushed down the 'to do' list.

It wasn't because we weren't committed to the idea. I was head over heels for Dan and he was the same for me, but we were both so insanely busy and the logistics of planning a wedding between a Welshman and an Aussie were tough. Wherever we decided to tie the knot, one half of our family and friends were going to have to fly for 24 hours just to see us say

'I do'. If we held our nuptials on Terrigal Beach in New South Wales, where I was from, or in a castle in Wales, where Dan had grown up (well, it was near a castle), there were serious air miles required. And then, to complicate things even further, I found out I was pregnant again. It was wonderful news and we were both ecstatic, but I didn't want to walk down the aisle looking wayward (and perhaps not so glamorous), so we put the idea of a big wedding aside, at least for the time being.

After what had happened last time, Dan and I decided not to tell anyone about our happy news and just relax into it. Good plan, or it was until I spoke on the phone with anyone, and I mean *anyone*, who asked how I was. I couldn't help myself – the words 'I'M PREGNANT' hurtled out of my mouth. Whoops! Dan just rolled his eyes as each caller was sworn to secrecy like the nation's security depended on it.

'I thought we weren't going to tell anyone until 12 weeks,' Dan quite rightly queried. 'That's only 14 people,' I replied defensively. After another eye roll

Dan said it'd be quicker if I let him know the people I hadn't told (lucky one of us is so practical!).

Being a bride has never really been a big deal to me – I've never chucked a 'Muriel' and tried on gowns or rings. I love a great frock, so it wasn't the shopping that put me off. It's just that none of my boyfriends had ever made me feel serious enough to imagine the 'ever after' bit. But Dan was different. I had such deep confidence that we were beyond any cliché of 'meant to be' and bringing a child into the world with this man just seemed to complete the perfect set.

With the wedding on hold and a baby on the way it was time to get on with planning how the hell the next bit was going to unfold. There were all the usual small-scale questions like:

'Can we still go on that holiday in September?'

and

'I wonder if I can still squeeze into that dress?'

And then there were the wider-ranging (and anxiety-provoking) questions like:

'Are we going to be able to afford all the stuff that comes with having and housing a baby?'

'Will we really get by without my wage?'

'For how long?'

And then there were the really big existential questions that most newly pregnant women wrestle with. You know the ones . . .

'Am I grown-up enough to be a mother?'

'Can I do this?'

'What if I stuff it up?'

My head was spinning thinking about it all. But with so much work booked for the year ahead I needed to focus on that and let the universe pull me along.

The next few weeks were seriously hectic. I was preparing to head off to the Vodacom Funny Festival in Cape Town, South Africa, for three weeks and I was still feeling strange thanks to my newly acquired knocked-uppery. There is something quite peculiar about those first few weeks of a pregnancy. It isn't just the thoughts I mentioned earlier that account for it, there are also the physical changes – I was sure everyone could see my tummy getting bigger (probably just nervous bloat). I couldn't believe men weren't giving up their seats to me on public transport, no matter how much mummy-tummy rubbing I engaged in. I don't know what they thought I was doing!

Before I left for Cape Town the most amazing phone call came through from my British agent, Janette (who was with PBJ, the most respected agency in the UK). I'd been one of ten people chosen from thousands of applicants to pitch a television show idea at the Montreal Just for Laughs Comedy Festival.

This was an enormous opportunity. Only a few festivals in the world are considered pinnacles of our business. The toast of the world's best festivals include Edinburgh and Melbourne, but the Montreal festival is what athletes would call an elite 'invitation meet'. You can't just turn up to this one – you have to be invited to take part in the big events – so I was over the moon.

The pitch that won the attention of the judges was an idea I had only just come up with – when I found out I was pregnant. The idea coincided with the cut-off date for the application so it all seemed meant to be. I am quite a lazy writer unless I have a deadline, which must be a hangover from my school days when I did all my homework the night before it was due to be handed in. I've always been a big fan of 'the last minute'.

When that little stick told me I was pregnant again it started me thinking about how I was going to earn money during and after the big event. Stand-up is not the ideal environment for a woman with child and at that time audiences were still allowed to smoke in venues. Trust me, there is nothing less relaxing than being pregnant on-stage in a high heel at 10.30 at night with 400 people blowing smoke directly at you. Needless to say finding another income source was a great idea, and submitting some TV proposals was the easiest way I could think of to earn money while still staying in the same industry. I hadn't had a 'real' job in more than ten years, so there wasn't much else I could do.

The working title of the show I came up with was: 'Is My Baby Gay?' Okay, I can already hear you tut-tutting and shaking your head but let me explain. There are so many theories surrounding what's good for your baby in utero, and of course for those vital first few years. What you eat, listening to classical music, early learning devices, baby sign language – the pressure for new parents is endless. So I wanted to explore whether there is a way to shape your child to gain certain qualities. Not just gay either. My plan was for a six-part series that would break down into 'Is my baby a rock star?', 'Is my baby an astronaut?', 'Is my baby an elite athlete?', 'Is my baby a porn star?' and so on. Through a combination of scientific research, talking to specialists, geneticists and to the parents who raised these particular 'stars', I'd find out whether it actually was the pre-birth Mozart, macrobiotic diet and flash cards that did it, or just plain old Mother Nature. The most exciting part of the whole experience was that I could present this idea as a pregnant woman. This was not only a case of serendipity but it meant I would look so incredibly committed to the project, a 'here is one I prepared earlier' type of scenario.

The downside to my inclusion in the pitching festival was I had to pay my own way to get there . . . and until Dan and I heard about the Montreal offer we'd been discussing baby budgeting and had decided we'd have to rein in our spending. But it was too big an opportunity to pass up, so we bought the ticket, booked the accommodation and the day after I flew home from Cape Town I was due to fly to Canada. I wasn't worried about the work or the pitch but I wasn't sure how I was going to cope for four weeks during this vital stage of gestational whingeing without Dan. Mmm. I felt sooky just at the thought of us being apart.

The weeks leading up to my departure seemed to take forever. Once I'd come to terms with the idea of no Dan I focused on what I had to look forward to and it was all not coming quickly enough for my liking. Cape Town was going to be the perfect respite from the British winter and after seeing the line-up of comics going with me I knew the festival was going to be heaps of fun.

Top of the list of reasons to be cheerful about Cape Town was that one of my all-time international favourites, Tina C, was going to be there. Tina is a six-foot-three super-glamorous country singing star from Tennessee who fills the Sydney Opera House annually. When the show's over and all the make-up's washed off, Tina turns back into Christopher Green, an Olivier Award-winning British actor and writer from North London. The second reason for going was Andrew Maxwell, a really cheeky Irish, political 'voice of the working class' type of comic who, whenever I work with him, seems to be on a mission to liberate everyone's minds using the power of intense laughter. The third plus was a very sweet old-school jazz saxophonist comic named Tony Gerrard, who had been wheelchair-bound since a bout of childhood polio. Then there was an older comic, who I can't possibly name and shame, but I call him Mr Pervy. Mr Pervy wore the same three-piece suit, complete with spats, for three weeks, regardless of the weather or activity. Spray-painting his bald spot with hair dye, he bragged on- and off-stage about still living with his mother even though he was in his 50s. He features nudie snaps of young ladies on his website so you can just imagine how much we had in common.

After Dan dropped me off at the airport, which in London is a sign of true love as it's an average of three hours each way (even if you live next door to the runway) thanks to the London traffic, I met up with the whole motley crew and we headed off like a gang of restless teenagers on a school excursion. I was armed with a suitcase full of fabulous gowns and matching shoes for the shows, and ample Juicy Couture terry-towelling dresses and trackies for those more casual days. I think I may have become involved with a Gottex strapless one-piece in chocolate and baby blue, but though the suit is memorable, the date is sketchy. Oh, and I always travel with sheepskin boots (something Pamela Anderson and I have in common).

(I like to tell you what was in my bag, clothes wise, as the very act of packing my favourite garments is my happy place. It will not have escaped your attention that I am quite a label freak, but I am reasonably confident it had nothing to do with my ongoing broke status. Anyway, I *needed* all of those things. Plus when you are performing you accumulate the odd designer something from the sales in the many different locations you travel through. Note: I am adding this point specifically for my accountant.)

Suitably attired and cheerfully packed, I was off. There is something so very satisfying about travelling in a group: it makes me feel rather smug during the flights, turning me into the sort of pest who heckles the safety instructions and asks questions about the validity of the life vest's light and whistle. So clever. Being with a pack gives me the sort of confidence in my own virtue that when I get up to go to the bathroom I make sure everyone in my section knows that I know someone in another aisle. And I take pleasure in pulling back the curtain to business class and revealing all the grumpy people who overpaid for a wider seat and a hot roll. I think you get the picture.

After we touched down, Cape Town felt like another world. I was nine weeks' pregnant and feeling like a million bucks. We were herded through customs and met by Cape Town's own Eddie Cassar, the guru PR. As the director of the festival Eddie was the sort of handsome, distinguished gentleman who couldn't do enough for us, which is such a weird change for comics as we are usually treated like elephant-men, who have to hang around in a storeroom till show time. Eddie and his family came to collect us like we were the international kings of comedy and, in turn, we all couldn't wait to make his festival a success.

I always like to think of myself as being up on world events (and am quite capable of headline-style statements that sound impressive at a dinner party after a few wines). I can kid myself this is true until I arrive in a place like South Africa and start to get an understanding of how much I don't actually know. I had researched all the basics about the country before I left London, so I was in the know about a few facts, like the population of approximately 3.5 million, the fact that Nelson Mandela was a political prisoner for more than 25 years on an island just off Cape Town's peninsula and that Aussies, New Zealanders and South

Africans were often grouped together as one big party gang in the UK, so on that point I was confident we would share some common ground.

The festival shows were in a big 600-seat theatre called the Baxter and I was booked to perform six nights a week for a gruelling 15 minutes. Stand-up can be quite full-on when the responsibility of the entire show rests on your shoulders so I was delighted to share the stage with my fellow travellers. We were all used to doing an hour of material, so limiting our gems to such a short time-frame was like being on a summer holiday. The audiences were so much fun and really got into the constantly sold-out shows. Stand-up is a reasonably new form of entertainment in South Africa, with the comedy festival only a little over ten years old at the time.

When dealing with a nation still smarting from the struggle against apartheid, I had to be on my best behaviour and not offend. Treading very carefully with my worldly opinions proved to be much harder than it sounds, although hardly a night went by when we wouldn't meet some white person in the foyer who rattled off a series of racist 'jokes' citing them as 'things you used to be able to say in the old South Africa'. It was very strange.

In our time off we went sightseeing around Cape Town. Because Chris Green and I are great friends we formed quite the 'modern' couple and spent all of our spare time together. (I don't think either of our boyfriends minded and it was not like he could accidently knock me up.) Of course we had to limit how far we travelled each day so we could be back for the show each night. Every morning we'd plot our little adventures and head off in our hire car. Nearly a week and a half into our stay we realised that Tony Gerrard had not really seen much of Cape Town at all. Being in a wheelchair hadn't restricted him as much as you would think and over the years he had toured around the world many times. On this trip, though, he seemed to be in a 'can't be bothered sightseeing' mode, so Chris and I decided to take him with us up the majestic Table Mountain, one of South Africa's most prominent landmarks.

Table Mountain is a flat-topped sandstone mountain overlooking Cape Town only accessible by cable car or hiking. The perfect destination for a wheelchair-bound man and a newly pregnant woman with the associated bladder issues. Christopher, Tony and I made our way to the cable car that would carry us just over 1086 metres into the air. Once we got to the top it made me nervous pushing Tony's wheelchair around because we were so high up and there were such steep drops on every side. The view was spectacular, as you can imagine, but the other tourists were so rude. People were barging in front of us at every turn, in case they were stuck behind the wheelchair. So we decided to have our own fun, at Tony's suggestion, by running the chair into the legs of anyone who pushed in front of us, then waiting to see their faces when they turned around to have a go, only to see Tony, a 50-year-old man in a wheelchair, smiling up at them. We laughed so hard that Tony reckons he nearly filled a bag.

I loved being part of the group but I did try to keep my distance from Mr Pervy, as whenever he could he singled me out for some extra-special sexual innuendo which I found particularly insulting. Let's just say our humour did not align. It wasn't too much of a hardship to stay away from him as my sense of smell was so heightened from pregnancy that his rancid body odour nearly made my eyelids peel back. The hardest part was when we were all in the car on our way to the theatre. I had to wind down the window and put my head out to stop from throwing up. The heady mix of baby powder, hair dye and disintegrating suit were more than I could cope with.

Most of the time I managed pretty well, but one particularly queasy morning we were all in the car on our way down the freeway to do some radio interviews and I had my head out of the window as usual, when disaster struck. The breeze was so strong that I had no time to react as my wire-framed, blue-tinged Chanel sunglasses were ripped from my head. I watched in horror as they catapulted under the wheels of the car travelling behind us. I was devastated, but then something happened that put my mourning over Chanel sunglasses into perspective.

Two weeks into my stay I woke up to the news that three bombs had gone off in central London. I knew Dan was working in the West End that week and he always travelled there by public transport. I felt a horrible, sinking sensation when I realised he could easily have been on a train or a bus at the wrong time and caught up in the terror. My only source of information was *Sky News* and the commentators and news reports echoed the horror we all felt during September 11. I tried calling Dan a million times but of course everyone else was doing the same (calling loved ones, not calling Dan) so all cellular communication was log-jammed and I couldn't reach him on his mobile.

I have to admit that I suffer from what I call 'death stress' even when there is no real threat apparent. I know being pregnant made it worse but even when I wasn't pregnant I would often think, 'Oh my God, what would I do if Dan was dead?' Gruesome, yes, but also really, really scary. These thoughts usually hit me if Dan is out late or if I haven't heard from him all day. My death stress was in full flight that day, but this time there was a logical reason for it.

Luckily Dan had the good sense to know I would be freaking out, so as soon as he could he called the hotel from a landline to put my mind at ease. I was beside myself with relief to hear from him and find out he was okay. He told me that the vibe in London was surreal. People were distressed at the fatalities and horrific injuries, but once the initial panic subsided most hardened Londoners he knew were just talking about how pissed off they were about the trains not working.

I remember when I first moved to London I kept hearing about how many people jump under the tube each week. Then one day I was travelling with one of my English friends when our train hit someone. My mate said, 'I am sorry for the poor guy who jumped, but how the hell am I supposed to get home to North Finchley now?' It bothered me then and as I listened to what Dan was saying I felt the same unease about it. But if I was sitting in unmoving traffic or crammed on a station platform I might feel the same.

Once I knew Dan was okay I let my panic go and Chris and I headed off to visit Robben Island, the site of Nelson Mandela's former prison which had become internationally known for its brutality during the apartheid years. I was already jittery and once we stepped foot on the island the stench of heartache and injustice was still very much in the air and it made my heart feel heavy.

Our tour guide was an ex-political prisoner who told us that when his father came to visit him, guards shot his father as he got off the boat in front of him as a punishment. I did not want to sob in front of this man who had been through a kind of hell I could barely imagine and my little corn-fed, white-bread existence could never have survived. I just let the tears roll silently down my cheeks as a mark of respect, while wondering how this could ever have gone on in my lifetime. He spoke of forgiveness and of 'Mr Mandela' who, following his release from prison in February 1990, had led the way to a national healing with his dignity and his ideas of reconciliation that helped create the 'new South Africa'. Walking around that place listening to the guide's stories was just too much for my pregnant, hormonally charged head. I can't even forgive someone who cuts in on my lane when I'm driving.

I'm glad I experienced Robben Island and learned what I did, but I was also happy to include more light-hearted excursions in this magical South African tour. I guess it isn't surprising that one of those excursions took us on a fabulous safari. Now when I say safari, don't put any time aside to be too impressed. Mind you, I did wear a superb pith helmet with a khaki combination shirt and Bermuda shorts so I looked the part but it was, in fact, just a big game-park zoo near Cape Town and not the wild South African veldt. We were driven around in the back of one of those open-top, four-wheel-drive glamour vans and were protected by gamekeepers as we went looking for the 'big five' (lion, African buffalo, African elephant, black rhino, leopard). It was a bumpy ride and I was thankful for the orange juice break halfway through.

We didn't have a performance that night, so after our post-safari dinner (where I think I ate all the big five) we repaired to the most luxurious cabins I have ever seen, each with a huge wraparound balcony where I came to understand why Paul Simon sings so passionately about being under African skies. When I looked up I was bedazzled. The night sky looked like a Vegas light show. I loved everything about being on safari, but sleeping in a four-poster bed by yourself can be so draining!

The three weeks flew by quickly and I was genuinely sad when my South African journey came to an end. But I was very happy that there was only an eight-hour flight separating me from Dan's arms (sigh!), even if I was only going to be home for 24 hours before flying to my next huuuge adventure in Montreal, for what I hoped would be the opportunity of a lifetime.

I packed my bags, met up with the group and we arrived at the airport relaxed, tanned and armed with our 'we are such a cool group' private jokes from our time spent together. After take-off the seatbelt sign finally pinged off, much to my delight as I was busting to go to the ladies. Why is it when you are busting to 'go' on a plane there is always a line to get in? Making small talk outside toilets has never been one of my favourite pastimes but finally it was my turn.

That was the moment I realised I was bleeding. Not just a few drops but really bleeding. I did the old teenage-girl trick of rolling several layers of toilet paper into a wad and placing it in my undies – sorry to be so graphic but I had no idea what was going on and hadn't thought I'd need to think about such supplies for at least another eight months. I was frightened and unsure what to do so I cleaned it up, left the toilet and found a flight attendant. She was very nice to me and explained that there were pads in the drawer of each bathroom . . . Pads . . . I could not believe I was having this conversation 20 minutes into an eight-hour flight. When I returned to my seat Andrew Maxwell made a joke about me picking up some trade in the bathroom and I very calmly replied, 'I think I'm having a miscarriage.'

Andrew is always a very sweet man but he was an absolute godsend during that flight. Even with his support those were some of the longest hours of my life. I had to keep returning to the bathroom every half-hour to sort myself out. I kept trying to convince myself I wasn't miscarrying, that I was just experiencing some adjustment bleeding. But I knew I was kidding myself. The hardest part was that I couldn't get in touch with Dan, who would have reassured me and made sense of the whole thing.

When we landed I couldn't wait to get home. I called Dan to tell him what was happening and that I'd get a cab. The rest of the trip was a blur.

Dan was waiting out the front of our place. Even though I was upset, seeing his face was like a million Christmas mornings rolled into one. As soon as I saw him I felt safe and knew I'd be okay. He gave me a big hug, took my bags upstairs and put me in the car to take me to the hospital. He'd contacted them and the antenatal staff were waiting for us.

After examining me, the look on the doctor's face told us it was all over. I just could not believe it. Everything had been fine and I'd had no hint of trouble, no pain and no clue that I was going to lose this baby. I didn't understand but there was no time to dwell on anything or start 'what if-ing'. I needed to make some quick decisions: I was offered the choice of a minor operation with a few days' recovery, or some tablets that I could take then go home and wait it out.

I must have been in shock because all I could think about was that in 24 hours I would be flying to Montreal. I had no time for any of this, but figured an operation was out of the question so the tablets had to be the way to go. I have no idea why I was being so pragmatic instead of exploding in tears like any normal person. I just wanted the weirdness to be over. I wanted to stop what was happening and go back in time a few days to when everything was fine.

If I thought the flight from Cape Town was a long, drawn-out process, it was nothing compared with the 12 hours after I left the hospital. I lay on the couch in our flat oscillating between complete devastation and out-of-context practicality, like wondering how I was going to find the time to have my roots done (well, the dark hair was growing quickly and I was looking like a bar of Top Deck chocolate).

At the same time, I was feeling useless and defective and sorry for myself and then I'd be furious that I'd just missed out on three weeks of South African sauvignon. It was an extremely odd time and the combination of my insane thoughts with the excruciating stomach and pelvis pains and the need to be on the toilet for about ten hours made me feel like I was not connected to the world around me at all.

I think you get some of the idea about the hell this was but, until then, when anyone had given me the news about their miscarriage, I'd not been even vaguely aware of what they had been through. Now I felt guilty that all I had ever offered was a paltry, 'You poor thing, are you okay?' But even now I think I would struggle; it is so hard to know the right thing to say.

Despite everything I was grittily determined to get on that plane to Montreal. I was damned if I was going to let this miscarriage ruin my career opportunity. So I pulled myself together, repacked my bags and even managed to have my roots done on the way to the airport the next evening.

Dan was so calm and supportive about all of my slightly off-centre decisions. He looked after me for the whole horrible miscarriage and then, knowing the trip was something I had to do for myself, drove me out to the airport. The only way I could keep going was to focus on Montreal, but it was a very sad farewell.

In all of the drama Dan hadn't had the chance to give me the surprise DVD he'd made for me to use during my pitch. It had taken him the best part of the three weeks I'd been away to hand draw and animate the opening credits for the show. He'd drawn a cartoon of a baby who transformed from genius to rock star to little Village Person to a whole heap of other things, all set to the old Eddie Cantor hit 'Yes Sir, That's My Baby'. He gave it to me just before I left and it was so funny and the perfect accompaniment to my presentation. I couldn't believe how amazing it was. I was set to blow those judges away.

Before I tell you about Montreal can we briefly talk about pads? I have not really been involved with them for years but the 'maternity' size I had to wear were more like surfboards than the skinny wing-bearing nothings you hear about during mealtimes on TV. It is very hard to feel sexy when you are walking with what feels like a load of washing between your legs. Too much information? Okay, let's get back to Montreal.

The Just for Laughs Festival was the perfect place to heal my spirit. My hotel was super glam and the industry vibe pervading the town was bursting with opportunity. After working in stand-up for more than 15 years (some might say since birth), I had the added advantage of knowing about 500 people there, so the whole event felt like a party week with old mates having lots of laughs and just a few late nights. (I even remember making myself available to the odd mojito as it seemed silly not to.)

I woke up on pitching day feeling way too over-excited which, after what had just gone on, was not the emotion I was expecting to feel. I had treated myself to a to-die-for Karl Lagerfeld black baby-doll chiffon, lace and satin dress and teamed it with a pair of killer silver, sparkly, skyscraper heels that would have made Dorothy jealous (let's say the outfit certainly took my mind off the surfboard).

The presentation was held in the ballroom of the Delta Hotel, the central meeting point for the festival, and it was filled with talent scouts, booking agents, producers, comedy commissioners, managers and agents from all over the world. The panel of judges for the pitching competition was made up of a series of TV network commissioners representing the USA, Canada and the UK.

There was to be no 'winner' for the pitching presentations, just the opportunity to have your project picked up and made by one of the networks. Sounds like winning to me. I was sixth in line to present so I had quite a while to wait and watch. Some presentations were really funny and some were just strange. It was hard not to get up and 'perform' the pitch to get laughs – getting an idea across and selling yourself in five minutes was quite the challenge.

Luckily for me the judges were very positive and Graham Smith from the Paramount Comedy Channel in the UK made an appointment for me to come and see him the second we both returned home. Everyone loved Dan's cartoon opening and I had the distinct impression my presentation was a hit.

The following few days were just like winning the lottery, with all sorts of people – from comedians to big agents – telling me how much they loved my pitch. I was on top of the world. The absolute highlight came on the last day when I was approached by a man named Bryan Scott from Picture This Television, the Emmy Award-winning, New York-based production company behind the hit television series *Kathy Griffin: My Life on the D-List.*

Bryan had seen me doing audience warm-ups in London for the series *The Kumars at No. 42* and that, combined with what he'd seen in Montreal, meant he wanted to offer me a 12-month development deal. To say I was shocked and elated would be the understatement of the millennium.

I couldn't fathom the emotional obstacle course of the previous seven days. I don't understand how I survived it still smiling. But I could feel the adrenaline wearing off and it was definitely time to go home.

I was returning to reality, but my reality was a life with love and support. I couldn't wait to get back. I may have had sexier shoes but Dorothy was spot-on when she said, 'There's no place like home.'

6

Vegas, Baby, Vegas

You know those people who always see the good in everything – the ones who can't help finding the silver lining all the time? That's Dan. God, it was good to see him again after the extreme emotional lows and highs of my travels. Talking on the phone is just not the same as being in the same room (or the same country!). As usual, the pace of our life together didn't slacken off. Almost straight away we left London to do some shows at my sixth Edinburgh Festival.

Soon afterwards we heard about a terrorist attack in the Egyptian city of Sharm el-Sheikh. I had the 'that is just dreadful' reaction most of us have, then went back to whatever I was doing at the time. I know it is awful but it is only human . . . we can't possibly absorb all the horror in the world and keep living if we focus on it. Can we? Two days after a series of bombs went off in this Red Sea holiday resort, ironically known as the 'City of Peace' due to the many international peace conferences held there, the normally high price to travel to Sharm el-Sheikh had dropped to an all-time low. The locals wanted things to get back to normal as quickly as possible and needed tourists to help them out.

Situated on the Sinai peninsula, 'Sharm', as it is affectionately known, is a dream destination for diving and sun enthusiasts. When Dan suggested we take advantage of the cheap fares and go on holiday there as the perfect antidote to our tiredness and sadness, I couldn't agree more. Like every September in London, the days were shortening and the reality of the British winter fast approaching, so the thought of bobbing around in the very same sea that had been parted by none other than that old funster Moses seemed like a top idea.

There is something extra special about a cheap flight out of the UK – the cheaper the flight the farther the airport usually is from your home. (You'd think I'd have learned the hard way after my earlier trip to Paris, but apparently not.)

I don't have great faith in airlines I've never heard of. I suspect it could be because every time one of them has a crash, they change their name to distance themselves from the bad PR. So I'll admit it did concern me that the only company flying to Sharm that week was called something like 'Pharaoh Air' and their flights were leaving from Gatwick.

Even though technically a London airport, Gatwick was three very 'relaxing' public transport hours away from our flat, so when we closed our front door we knew we were in for a long day. Getting across London is a chore at the best of times, but dragging a bag full of your favourite summer dresses up and down the steps of several tube lines past crowds of grumpy commuters is what I consider an extreme physical challenge. However, thoughts of sun, sea, the chance to wear a fetching sunfrock and imbibe a few holiday mojitos were all the motivation I needed to battle on.

Imagine our surprise when we arrived at the airport to find our flight had been delayed. Now the perfect way to soothe already frazzled nerves is not to hang around the relatively underdeveloped Gatwick airport for eight hours before getting on a five-hour flight. There is not a lot to do at this place while you wait – there's a newsagency, a shop for duty-free ciggies, booze and sunglasses and a bar serving beer, tea and the odd toasted sandwich. But if I have to be stuck anywhere I want it to be with Dan.

Being such frequent travellers we always find a way to pass the time (Yahtzee, think Yahtzee). At Gatwick we kept ourselves amused by daring each other to go back and forth through security sporting different types of moustaches we'd drawn on our faces with a pen, to see if we'd be stopped. I must say, I did get some admiring glances for my Mardi Gras-style handlebar but I faded into the background when Dan, who won the challenge, went through the full security procedure wearing what I dubbed 'the Bic

Hitler' with absolutely no response from the staff. Too superb. International British airport security won't let you board the plane with a nail file but impersonating Hitler is fine (except if you are Prince Harry).

Finally, after what seemed like days, we arrived at Sharm, described in the guide books as the 'Egyptian Riviera'. It was as magnificent as you'd imagine the ultimate oasis to be, complete with Bedouins and colourful tents between the mountains and the sea. Our resort was utterly palatial, with groovy villas, several restaurants and quite a few pools with private areas in which to tan or read if you just wanted to be on your own. Dan and I rarely mix much with other people when we are away on holidays together. I guess it is a part of our unwinding process. We spend so much of our daily and performing lives giving out lots of personality, so when it comes time to have a break we tend to drop away from any social interaction. (Maybe we are just a bit shy, who knows?) Either way, this party of two is the ultimate break for me.

The only downside to this super-cheap holiday was that, sadly, the hotel was full of pigs. Now I do appreciate how elitist this sounds and as a girl from Gosford you might think I have just a little of the pot-calling-the-kettle-black syndrome going on, but you must understand we were in a location that only a week before had been considered one of the more expensive and exclusive holiday destinations in the world. After the terrorist bomb attacks, it wasn't just Dan and I who took up the cheap offers. But I don't think the locals quite expected the clientele a cheap holiday offer would bring (I know Dan and I didn't). The hotels were filled with what I can only describe as rough British women with their tits out who were focused on ordering 'cold hard screw' cocktails at the top of their voices oblivious to the very strict religious traditions those serving them adhered to.

So when I say the hotel was 'full of pigs', I really mean full of women who openly flirt with men used to seeing no more than a woman's face and who use their meal breaks to pray. Any promenade around any pool would have a bevy of women 'sunny side up' and it just didn't feel right. There is a time and a place for 'shake 'em baby, you won't break 'em', but this was not one of them and as one of their gender I felt ashamed.

Despite the occasional raucous intrusion that drifted our way as we swam, read and slept, Dan and I settled into the holiday vibe. But it seemed all our conversations kept coming back to the subject of our wedding and the same old obstacles reared their heads: when and where we could possibly have it to make it fair for all our family and friends. I don't remember whether it was Dan or me who finally said, 'We should just go to Vegas and get married on New Year's Eve and whoever can come can come', but we both laughed hysterically at the thought. And then we realised it was a great idea and became really excited. We decided to fly the idea past our family and friends when we got home and see how they reacted. The rest of our holiday was spent giggling at the thought of Elvis marrying us while trying to keep away from all the holidaymakers from hell.

Back in London, we were straight on the phone to everyone. Bingo. They loved the idea. Once you are out of your early twenties, it can be hard to find a great way to celebrate New Year's Eve, so the thought of a party in Vegas sounded like the perfect plan. I can't imagine it was the dream wedding my parents had in mind for their only daughter but they had waited 37 years to see me walk down the aisle, and so as long as the ceremony did not involve Elvis (hmmmm), they were happy to take it all in their stride.

Now that we had a plan, we needed to make it a reality. We had about three months to organise a wedding in America from our home in London that would see people of diverse ages and social expectations arrive from Australia, various parts of the US and Wales. Easy . . . and at least I had something to distract myself from the weather!

Since I'd arrived in the Mother Country I'd struggled with the onset of winter. It arrives quickly and I always found it gruelling. The days grow progressively darker until, by the end of October, the light is nearly gone by 3.30pm. It has to be one of the most difficult aspects of British living for Aussies. I have heard it called temperature depression, the winter blues or SAD (seasonal affective disorder) but whatever you want to call it I had it and that's exactly how it feels. Like you are carrying a sack of sadness with you. Coming from a country that seems to have never-ending sunshine to a country with very little is enough to make anyone feel a bit down and certainly adds to the general homesickness most Aussies feel. It doesn't mean you love one place more than the other; it is just different and hard to adjust to.

Most people I know throw themselves into equal amounts of working, sleeping and drinking to get through the worst of the winter months. Some even do all three at the same time but I only had time for one.

I was working like a slave doing London gigs in between touring around the country with Ardal O'Hanlon as the support on his massive UK tour. After playing Father Dougal on the BBC hit comedy *Father Ted*, Ardal had built up such a devoted following that the theatres were full every night. Not just full, but to the brim with the most lovely audiences, who were all there determined to get as many laughs out of the evening as they could. It sounds strange to say that an audience is at a stand-up show to laugh as much as possible, but you'd be surprised at how many people seem to come along with no intention of laughing at all.

It's not always the audience's fault that a giggle is hard to come by. There are so many factors that can spoil a show before it even starts. Is the theatre set up okay? Have some of the audience had an aggressive day? Were the front-of-house staff rude while seating everyone? How good is the lighting? How comfy are the seats? And my all-time favourite potential laugh killer, how clear is the sound? If the theatre is too light or hot or even too wide it is easy to lose the concentration of the crowd and, in turn, lose the room. Ardal was a seasoned and fabulous stand-up, having toured for many years before his television career went through the roof, so he had not only picked the best theatres possible but some of the best hotels too. We went from resort to resort, crisscrossing the country, lapping up the best of British hospitality from Norfolk to Brighton, Worcester to Manchester, Cardiff to Aberdeen and beyond.

When I'm on tour I'm the worst friend as I seem to get lost in the immediacy of 'just getting through today' and forget about everyone else. Most of my mates are used to me not returning calls so when I do resurface we catch up and pick up where we left off. Over the years I have lost a few buddies who think I can't be bothered with them, when in actual fact there is so much more going on. I am either just arriving home from tour, on tour or getting ready to go on tour. I do listen to the messages on my voicemail but I have to confess that they leave my head as I rush to get ready and leave for the next journey. Trying to organise a wedding with a woman who is notorious for not looking past a 24-hour block isn't easy, but somehow Dan coped with it all.

I was in full tour mode – up early each morning, checking out of whatever hotel I'd been in the night before, driving the several hours to the next hotel with Ardal and the tour manager, checking in, doing a workout in the gym to try to lose a bit of pre-bridal beef, showering, blowdrying and trowelling on make-up before going to a sound check at the theatre. Doing the show was the highlight of the day, before having a late dinner and hitting the sheets, dreaming of missing the wake-up alarm that started the 'groundhog day' feeling, bright and early the next morning. This went on for two and a half months and I was feeling progressively more shattered.

My leg of the tour ended in Belfast, where I had already spent a good deal of time. The BBC in Northern Ireland has a really creative comedy department and over the years I had been lucky enough to take part in a number of their shows. When I was in Belfast I always stayed in the Europa Hotel, which is famous for being the most bombed hotel in Europe!

One night after the gig I managed to catch up with some comics who all happened to be staying at the Europa too. Time seemed irrelevant until, with plenty of wine under my belt, I realised that room service had closed. I was starving, so I took it upon myself to go out and get us all some pizzas. Excusing myself, I made my way across the road to the renowned pizza joint opposite the hotel.

On my way back, having spoken to everyone in the shop with the kind of enthusiasm only alcohol or a personality disorder brings, I spotted one of those semi-armoured police vans. Knocking on the window of the driver's door I asked the boys if they fancied a slice of Belfast's finest 'ham and pine'. They looked a little shocked at first but upon hearing my Aussie accent their alarm seemed to dissolve.

When I got back to the hotel and told my mates of my encounter with the local fuzz they were open-mouthed with shock. They told me that before the peace agreement was signed a few years earlier I might have been shot, or at the very least arrested, for even approaching a police van in such a casual way, especially carrying an unknown object. Women were known to have been used as terrorist decoys to kill police. I guess spotting my Anna Sui baby-doll mini and Chanel two-toned heels they figured I looked too silly to be on some pre-planned suicide mission.

Coming from a place like Australia that has no concept of political unrest and everyday terrorist acts, I always found it hard to understand that level of heightened alert. I am blessed that this is the case. Admittedly I had only ever been exposed to the more glam parts of Belfast and it always felt safe and calm to me.

Northern Ireland plays host to a number of comedy festivals and I had taken part in many of them over the years. One year I got to share a bill with Jimeoin in Omagh, a town sadly infamous for an Irish Republican Army bombing in 1998.

I never think it appropriate to ask locals about an event like that but I was curious and wanted to know the details. One lady I met who was open about what happened told me that the car carrying the explosives was meant to be driven to the town hall but the driver chickened out and parked it a way down the road. When the call was made to clear the town hall, many of the people who ran towards supposed safety actually put themselves in the impact zone where the car was parked. That one bomb killed 29 people, including a woman pregnant with twins, and injured hundreds more. It seems trite to say we don't know how lucky we are in Australia but when I'm in places like Belfast or Robben Island, where there has been such civil unrest and heartbreak, it is the first thing I think of.

Like a lot of people living in places of suffering, Belfasters know how to enjoy themselves. The shows with Ardal were a deafening success with screaming laughter and tumultuous applause. For me it was a really exciting night topped off by the great pleasure of meeting Ardal's father, who had driven up from Dublin. Dr O'Hanlon is the speaker in the Irish House of Commons and was not only fascinating to speak to but it turned out we had something rather unusual in common.

Before I tell you what that coincidence was, I will admit I am what the Irish refer to as a 'Plastic Paddy'. While very proud of the Irish bloodlines on both sides of my family, it was only in Ireland that I began to realise I knew very little about my lineage at all. I could quite easily spurt out a list of facts and locations about my family and the branches of my family tree but they were just words and it all felt disconnected from me. For example, my grandmother's brothers were killed by the Black and Tan army when she was a very young woman. She moved to London and then took a job as a lady-in-waiting for what turned out to be a nasty old woman. After a few months of working for the old beast, they both sailed to Australia. Now that I was spending time in Ireland those facts came to life and shone a metaphorical spotlight on so much of the story that I knew nothing about.

My biggest claim to Irish fame had always been that I am the great-great niece (once or twice removed) of the Countess Constance Markiewicz. My grandmother spoke of the Gore-Booth family link when I was growing up. I knew the Countess was a bit of a spunk as Yeats wrote extensively of her and her sister Eva's beauty (he wrote the poem 'In Memory Of Eva Gore-Booth And Con Markiewicz' in their honour, 'two girls in silk kimonos, both beautiful, one a gazelle') but when Ardal's father learned of my distant Irish connection, he told me that the story of

Constance Gore-Booth, the Countess of Irish freedom, is one that young girls searching for history's female heroes should all know. After what he told me I decided I wanted to know more about her.

According to Wikipedia (don't you love the internet!), Constance was born into a wealthy Irish family in London in 1868. Her dad was an explorer and philanthropist and he was known as a good bloke and model landlord in County Sligo. Having been raised by parents who were concerned for others not so well off surely shaped how Constance and her sister Eva would conduct their later lives. They might have been born with silver spoons in their mouths but they would soon spit those spoons out to go to work for the cause of Irish independence.

Eva became an activist for basic labour rights and women's suffrage in England and Constance would become the most famous woman of the Irish revolutionary movement. She was given a death sentence after being busted as one of the leading rebels in the Easter Rising. (This 'rising' was an attempt by militant Irish republicans to win independence from Britain, but obviously it was unsuccessful and its leaders were court-martialled and executed. It did, however, succeed in bringing republicanism back to the forefront of Irish politics.) Constance was apparently furious to find out that her execution would be reduced to prison time due to the fact that she was a woman. (I have to say this is one instance when I would have pulled the 'I am only a female' card.) She famously told the officer who brought her the news, '. . . I do wish your lot had the decency to shoot me'. She was a champion.

As it turns out, Dr O'Hanlon's seat in the Irish parliament is beneath a beautiful portrait of the Countess, so she is a part of his life nearly every day. Hearing about this amazing woman and her contribution to effecting massive change in Ireland, I wanted to bask in our connected bloodlines and share her glory, but comparing national hero status to travelling the world telling a few gags doesn't really match up. Just knowing we are remotely related made me feel weirdly good about myself. (I love my ego's ability to transfer a distant relative's achievements into my own glory – now that's truly Australian!)

While I was gallivanting around Ireland working and brushing up on my family tree, Dan kept himself busy in London, juggling the wedding preparations, freelancing as an advertising account director, trying to complete end-of-year works for his course at Central Saint Martins College of Art and Design all while doing stand-up at night. (Let's face it, he is so lazy!) But seriously, we were pushing ourselves hard and it was inevitable as the wedding came closer that one or both of us would get sick. There must be something like Murphy's Law that covers this, surely.

I was the one who crumbled. My sickness hit on Christmas Eve, the night before we were due to fly to LA. I had one of those sore throats where you are sure that some sort of animal has crawled in there and died. I didn't sleep too well and by 8am on Christmas Day I had to go to the emergency department of our local hospital – I felt like my throat was closing over and I was about to suffocate. It was very relaxing in the waiting room gasping for breath, knowing I had a flight at 3 o'clock that afternoon.

Have I ever told you how mad I am for a drip? I think it's the way that plastic bit hangs, speared into the top of your hand like some kind of badge of honour, that I like. As soon as the drip is attached you can look at anyone who might have doubted just how sick you really are with a smug, wan look. You have the bag to prove it. Getting to that point, the sticking it in and flicking it to get the fluid moving is vile and I try to pretend I am not there for that part.

The hospital doctor diagnosed me with a severe form of viral pharyngitis (most people know it by its colloquial name 'sore throat', but I think the proper medical term lends it more gravitas and is more appropriate to how ghastly I felt). The doctor tried to talk me into postponing our flight but through tears and some slobbering on my part I explained about my planned wedding and against his better judgement he filled me with drip-fed antibiotics, kept me under surveillance for a few hours then sent us off to the airport. Dan knows better than to try to stop me when I have my mind set on something, so he just steered me in the right direction. By the time I reached the departure gate I felt like I needed the last rites, not a boarding pass.

The flight was a delirious blur, but arriving in LA is always exciting. Flying in over the Hollywood sign will never be passé for me and as sick as I was, my heart insisted on skipping a beat (or maybe that was because I was so ill). Dan and I had been frequent visitors to the US since we'd met and it had become one of our favourite shopping and holiday destinations. California always seemed to be sunny, glamorous and offered up the possibility of instant wealth and success, at least initially. That feeling of opportunity masked the stench of too much heartache on the city streets but it was easy to be blinded to that other side. LA is basically 'fly paper' for anyone who wants to be in motion pictures and it's all anyone can talk about.

Every time Dan and I visited California, we stayed with the British couple who had introduced us years before. Jules and Crispin are easily two of the more spectacular people on the planet. They are one of those couples who are funny, super bright and beautiful looking. (Sometimes God is very unfair giving all of the good qualities to only a few.)

Jules and Crispin live in a superb open-plan glass and timber treehouse with a 360-degree view overlooking the lush green canopy of Laurel Canyon. The only other house we could see from their place was Justin Timberlake's compound. Just being there made me feel cool. Their place on Hermit's Glen ran off the famous Wonderland Avenue, a tree-lined street halfway up the canyon that had been host to a rich history of controversial and out-there events, including the 'Wonderland Killings' and the making of various rock videos, and it was the primary setting for Doors manager Danny Sugerman's memoir *Wonderland Avenue: Tales of Glamour and Excess*. Even though purchasing low-fat milk and gluten-free bread is not remotely like scoring cocaine or flirting with a rock star I still loved feeling that Laurel Canyon history every time I went to the local Canyon store. I am sure Jim Morrison would have ventured in there once or twice.

Dan and I had planned to have a few days to relax and unwind by hanging out at a few of our favourite spots in LA, like Mel's Diner on Sunset, Skybar at the Mondrian and Urth Caffé in WeHo (West Hollywood, I write with a smug insider's flourish), then do a bit of shopping at the Grove and Santa Monica before 29 December, when we were scheduled to head to Vegas in some hilarious V20 four-wheel-drive.

Sadly, these best laid plans were not to be. The flight hadn't helped my ailing health, surprisingly, and I ended up bedridden for four days with no obvious improvement even after sleeping most of the time. Our wedding was looming ever closer but I was fading away, so Dan insisted it was time to see a doctor. I'm sure you've heard over the years how difficult and expensive it can be to get medical attention in America but in LA, if you are in 'the industry' there are places you can go.

Jules suggested we try the Bob Hope Medical Center. Apparently they restrict themselves to only actors and performers (if I wasn't so ill I would have laughed because I had the impression everyone in

LA was an actor or performer). Dan rang and the conversation went a little like this:

Receptionist: 'Good morning, The Bob Hope Medical Center, how may I direct your call today?'

Dan: 'Oh, yes, good morning, my wife and I are here from London and she is very ill. My friend sees Dr So-and-So in your centre and suggested I call in the hope that she can see someone today.'

Receptionist: 'Is your wife an actor, Sir?'

Dan: 'Ah, yes she is and she is a comedian as well.'

Receptionist: 'Right, is she a SAG [Screen Actors Guild] member, Sir?'

Dan: 'No, but she is an Equity member in the UK.'

*Receptionis*t: 'Are you travelling with a showreel, press clippings or a biog and head-shot, Sir?'

(There was a slight pause here as Dan struggled with the direction the conversation had taken. He couldn't believe what he was hearing.)

Dan: 'Ah, yes, we do have a copy of her showreel with us as she is on her way to New York in a few weeks to do some work with a production company there and I'm sure I can access some of her press on the internet.'

Receptionist: 'Okay, Sir, well if you could print out some of the clippings and bring her showreel with you, the doctor can see her at 11am.'

Can you believe she hadn't even asked what was wrong with me? After a minor NTSC vs PAL panic that the showreel would not be compatible with the reception DVD player, Dan got everything sorted and just to be sure took his laptop with him. He helped me to the car and we set off to audition for the doctor (too bizarre).

After a quick viewing of the four-minute multi-edit of some of my greatest hits, I was asked to go to Treatment Room 3 and informed that the doctor would be right with me. (Thank God for the appearance of Eric Bana, dressed as Ray Martin, interviewing me dressed as Anna Nicole Smith and revealing a stunt plastic nipple in a *Full Frontal* sketch. I think Eric sealed the deal and secured my consultation.)

The doctor entered the treatment room like one of the Marx Brothers (I am not joking), using a voice you'd think would normally be reserved for three-year-olds. As soon as I heard 'Sooo what's wong wiv yooo den?' bizarrely I felt instantly on the mend!

I told him about my imminent wedding, described what had gone on over the past week, then showed him the medication I'd been given in the UK. He picked up the British medicine, let out a little laugh and lobbed it into a bin in the corner. Then he examined me.

After looking down my throat he used his big boy voice and told me that I had a basic 'strep throat' and it was time for some 'real' medication, in fact, the best that private healthcare can buy. He started me on a course of steroids – cool, if they work for Rambo then they work for me. The doctor added that I'd be feeling better by nightfall and then wished me good luck for the wedding. I found it hard to believe I would be feeling better so soon considering my level of incapacity, but I thanked him, and Dan and I headed back to Laurel Canyon.

Well, throw me over an ant hill and smear my ears with honey, by 8pm I was up playing my third game of Yahtzee, making myself available to a margarita and truly feeling all better. I strongly advise getting into AMA-approved medical drugs . . . they totally rock!

The next day, feeling like I had never actually been sick, Jules and I headed out to LAX to pick up Flic, who had travelled nearly 50 hours from Broome to be at my wedding. Once we had Flic with us we made our way to One Night Affair, a massive showroom where I had organised to hire my wedding dress.

Most brides-to-be might think I'm a bit of a skank hiring my gown, but the thought of spending so much money on a dress that you can only wear for one day makes me feel a little dizzy. I would much rather drop a few grand on some fabulous little black Narciso Rodriguez number that I can wear over and over again, rather than on some white catastrophe that makes me feel like I'm sitting on top of a quilted toilet roll.

The truth is I had already bought a lovely dress in London, months before. It was a very simple winter-white pleated chiffon and crepe cocktail-length dress I planned to team with a full-length cream faux sable and a silver Louboutin heel, but once I got to LA and thought about it some more it all just seemed a bit Hey-Mr-DJ-Madonna-ghetto-chic, so I changed my mind. Isn't that the bride's prerogative?

At One Night Affair I ended up modelling about 20 dresses in front of Jules and Flic. Nothing could compare to their reaction when they saw me in the strapless, lightly crystalled, full-circle-skirted brand-new Balenciaga that had arrived from Paris days before. Hello? Hire? Magnificent. They even lent me jewels and a simple Vera Wang veil, so I was set and ready to be the full bride without having to take out a bank loan to pay for the dress. I felt a million bucks.

The next morning we all bundled into the massive four-wheel-drive we'd hired and started out on the road to Vegas, laughing, squealing and carrying on, with the rule that the two people in the front were in charge of music and driving and the three in the back had to cope with being slightly suffocated by the meringue frock lying lovingly on our laps.

Driving across California to get to Vegas can be fun. For the first hour or so it was, but then I started getting restless and the dress was feeling heavy (I was obviously one of the people in the back). We resisted stopping to grab a snack until well into the second or third hour so we had something to look forward to. It was the only highlight for about 300 kilometres.

After driving for four hours we made it to Nevada and some casinos appeared on the horizon. At first they were spread out and quite small, then they were slightly bigger and I started to think, 'Is this it? I thought it was bigger than this.' I wasn't as annoying as the kid who constantly says, 'Are we there yet?', but I was close. I couldn't help myself and started to say things like:

'I don't remember it looking like this.'

'Where is the strip?'

'It's not that impressive.'

'This can't be it? Maybe it's the old part of Vegas?'

'Where is the pyramid thing?'

'Hang on, this is shit.'

I didn't know we were passing through one of the little daggy Nevada satellite casino towns catering to those who can't afford to lose their life savings in the real Vegas.

As we hurtled back into the blackness of the desert I realised my mistake and shut up. We drove another half an hour on a rollercoaster of hills and valleys through the desert until we reached the crest of yet another hill and hit an insane traffic jam that looked like a 10-kilometre snake made out of red tail-lights.

The delay made the fifth and final hour of the drive an agonising crawl. Our exuberance had waned and the dress seemed less meringue and more deadweight. We reached the peak of the last mountain and then we saw it . . . the real Las Vegas. It was like a current of electricity passed through all of us and excitement bubbled again despite our exhaustion and numb bottoms. There it was, rising like a strobing phoenix out of neon flames. I couldn't help grinning like Vince Vaughn . . . 'Vegas, Baby, Vegas!'

7

With this Ring . . .

Getting married in Vegas at the Little Church of the West meant Dan and I were in illustrious company (or dubious, depending on how you looked at it). Just some of the people whose footsteps we were following in were:

Angelina Jolie and Billy Bob Thornton

Richard Gere and Cindy Crawford

David Cassidy and Kay Lenz (admit it, if you were an Australian teenager in the '80s you loved *The Partridge Family*)

Gregg Allman

Shirley Bassey

Deanna Durbin

James Farentino

Red Foxx

Judy Garland

Bob Geldof

Zsa Zsa Gabor and one (possibly more) of her husbands

Betty Grable

Dudley Moore

Mickey Rooney and one (possibly more) of his wives

Telly Savalas

Heather Thomas

and

Billie Piper.

Sure, hardly any of these marriages lasted but that doesn't mean they weren't in love on the day, so I'm not going to judge. Besides, Dan and I were different . . . we had nothing to sign a pre-nup for.

After much consideration we booked the Deluxe Package #3 for our wedding, which came in at the bargain price of US$345. Now for anyone who thinks this a tad extravagant, wait till you hear what it included: the chapel fee; a rose bouquet for me; a boutonnière for Dan (I wasn't exactly sure what this was until the day but it sounded great. Oh . . . it is the lapel flower, not a pirate . . .); a dedicated church organist (no cheap tape-recording for us funsters); a customised wedding certificate and licence holder; a few snaps; a DVD recording of the ceremony that came with a five-minute history of the chapel; and live streaming of the service on the internet so family and friends around the world who couldn't make the trip to Vegas could watch our special moment. The only other cost was the minister's fee (a cash donation of $50 or more was recommended), so as far as I was concerned, for a 15-minute ceremony, the cashed-up minister was laughing like a shark in a kids' pool, *kerrrrching*.

It was going to be quite cosy – our family and friends, and about 500 000 other visitors spending New Year's Eve 2005 on the famous Las Vegas Strip. You can only imagine how insane the city was. It was an agoraphobic breeding ground and the sad part was that after spending an hour in the neon and noise I was over it. Yes, I am an idiot. What was I expecting? I hadn't considered what it would mean to be part of a huge throng in a location as manic as Las Vegas. I'd been too excited about our wedding to look beyond that.

The 36 of us taking part in the wedding festivities had all booked into the MGM Grand for four days. I thought it would be stupendous. While the horse pills were still working their magic and I was feeling great, whenever we ventured out of our room it was like queuing at the turnstiles at an Olympic Games opening ceremony. There were thousands and thousands of people everywhere and can I just say the selection of tracksuits was outstanding (so perhaps there actually was an Olympic convention going on . . . though the body shapes under the tracksuits tended to make me think not).

I know my family and friends were a bit shell-shocked on the first evening. We were our own little United Nations, with representatives not just from the classic locations like New York, London and LA, but also from Wales, Nigeria, Broome and Gosford, with every one of them ready for just one or two fun times despite the culture shock. We all met at the Wolfgang Puck restaurant for dinner and drinks and 787 000 dry Napa whites later everyone in the restaurant was new best friends. My aversion to Vegas evaporated as quickly as the liquid in my wine glass.

The next day, with substantial hangovers in place, Dan and I dragged ourselves out of bed to do our last-minute wedding chores. We headed across town into 'Old Vegas', the location of the County Hall, to get our marriage licence. I have no idea how couples supposedly get pissed and accidentally 'get hitched' in Vegas, when in fact the process is quite lengthy.

While you don't need a blood test like they say in the movies, the three-hour wait in line to buy the licence would allow most mortals ample time to sober up and get the hell out of there if they were having second thoughts. I mentioned earlier that if I have to wait anywhere with anyone, then please let it be Dan. We had a superb time people-watching from our spot in the queue. There were more freaky looks than a fashion week and I'll just say if you were without a Cuban heel and cowboy hat, you were nowhere. Dan and I felt extremely underdressed.

After a big morning of queue-standing and paperwork we were starving, so we stopped for lunch just near an old Vegas favourite, the Golden Gate Casino, where we found a strange little diner shaped like the interior of a train. After we propped our jackets and bags up on the handy overhead shelf, Dan got stuck into his 'Southern Pacific' and I inhaled my 'Achison Topeka', both with chips. All aboard. With my hangover overpowered by protein and trans fat, I felt like a new woman by the time I was finished.

We spent the rest of our wedding eve shopping for booze and MP3 speakers for the after-wedding party, then met up with everyone for another special group event.

Beforehand, if you had asked me to describe how I would spend the night before my wedding, I doubt the word 'bowling' would have come up. Spa treatment, yes; luxurious massage and lots of champagne, yes; bowling shoes, no. I know, I know . . . we were in Vegas and we went bowling!

The thing is, I don't gamble. I never have. Well, that is not entirely true. In 1984, when I was 16, I went to the Wyong races for the day with some school friends. We thought we were so chic, dressed in hats and our best outfits (which in my case was a Stuart Membery Edelweiss story skirt and matching sloppy joe, teamed with a navy penny-in-the-slot Milano brogue). Well, that day I managed to lose my entire savings of $16.77 betting in the bookies' ring. I put my trust in a self-concocted system based on the colour of the jockey's silks and it failed.

I was so dark about losing my money that I swore it would never happen again and I have not gambled a single cent from that day to this. Hmmmm, now that I think about it, the choice of Vegas as a holiday destination does seem a little redundant given my aversion to gambling (let's just put it down to me being a nice girl but, really, not very bright).

Anyway, that explains why we were bowling. And can I say sending those massive balls down the blue neon lanes was weirdly soothing and the sugar-based hot dog didn't hurt either. By the time we returned to the hotel I couldn't believe it was just one more sleep until our big day.

Waking up in a massive suite overlooking the Las Vegas Strip has a way of making you feel like George Clooney – even if you are a woman. With a view from the gold Mandalay Bay to the magnificent Wynn, we had gone way over our budget, but it was one of the sexiest views in the world, so more than worth it. The spa in the bathroom was full of an obscene number of bottles of wine and champagne, the living room was set up for the party and my dress was hanging in the walk-in robe ready for action.

I had always been impressed by Deborra-Lee Furness having two outrageously handsome 'man-maids' instead of bridesmaids when she married Hugh Jackman. I thought it was the coolest thing ever. So, as an homage to Deborra-Lee, I too chose a very handsome man-maid, my bestie Juzzy.

Early that afternoon a few girlfriends, my man-maid and my mum all came to the suite to help fold me into my dress and after a champagne (or two) we were ready to make our way down to the Bridal Stretch Hummer. Dan made himself scarce just as the bridegroom is supposed to do.

Have you ever heard such a ridiculous expression? The 'Bridal Stretch Hummer'. It sounds like a rude sex game but in fact it's an 18-seater high-mobility multipurpose wheeled vehicle. I felt that when one is a bride in the United States of America it seems silly not to travel to the fake church in the very symbol of ecological irresponsibility. It was a rainy, windy afternoon and where better to shelter my bridal self and my entourage than a party on wheels.

The journey to the Little Church of the West took us past the famous 'Welcome to Fabulous Las Vegas, Nevada' sign and in no time we had caught up with the groom's stretch Hummer. Can you imagine how silly we looked making faces and blowing kisses between cars? There was no mooning due to the presence of my mother, but the feeling was merry. At precisely 5.45pm we bundled into the tiny log cabin posing as a chapel and took our places.

We had chosen black tie as our dress code so everyone looked very dapper but, apart from Dan, my father looked the most handsome. He had been waiting for this moment for so long and was bursting with pride and excitement. I hadn't expected to be so emotional. Our choice to hold the wedding in Vegas was all about the party, but when 'Here Comes the Bride' started playing on the portable Roland organ in the corner and Dad and I stepped down the aisle it was overwhelming and I felt amazingly special. Of course I couldn't help myself and did a few 'celebrity waves' on my way (the celebrity wave is simply raising your arm above your head and splaying your fingers while maintaining a top-and-bottom-teeth-displaying smile) and the guests laughed on cue.

When I reached Dan, the look on his face was so beautiful that I did one of those extra breaths that is a cross between a hiccup and a cry. We were both beaming with love and joy as the 50-buck minister began the official ceremony.

We immediately understood why this was a 15-minute ceremony, as the minister spoke without pausing or taking a breath. He recited it all so quickly that the entire congregation of our family and friends got the giggles. The only words any of us could understand were Dan and Julie . . . who the hell is Julie? You'd think when you paid for the Deluxe Package #3 that he'd be able to get the bride's name right at least.

Despite feeling like we were stuck on fast-forward, everything was going fine. Or it was until we'd nearly finished the vows, when Dan committed the biggest faux pas of his life.

I hope the way I've described Dan so far means you don't think I've been exaggerating about how great he really is. As a relatively cynical, feminist, street-wise comedian, I would have no qualms bagging a man when he deserves it, but Dan just isn't one of those men. As far as I can see (and I've been looking for many years) he is perfect. He treats me, my family, his family and all of his and my friends with love and respect; he is hilarious and clever and, to top it all off, he is a spunk, *schwing*. So for Dan to make even a tiny faux pas during the ceremony was way out of character.

Admittedly I had started the ball rolling by saying 'for richer or much richer' earlier on in the vows, but Dan well and truly topped that when the minister said, 'Dan, would you please take Julia's ring', and my husband-to-be turned briefly to face 'the crowd' and said, 'I already have.'

There was a moment of awkward silence and then huge booming laughs filled the chapel. Realising exactly what he'd uttered, Dan was so horrified that he turned back again to our family and friends and said, 'I haven't you know, I haven't.'

Time was ticking away and I knew how mortified he was, so I lovingly leaned over to him and said, 'Do you mind if we wrap up the arse jokes and get on with the wedding?' The blood drained from his face as we were officially announced husband and wife. (The blood draining was not because we were officially married, it was because he was re-running the joke in his mind. Just so we are clear.)

We were given a DVD of the ceremony and of course, with the internet-streaming, loads of family and friends overseas got to see our vows live, but to this day Dan still can't watch it. He says he's sure that if you turn the volume up and listen closely enough, you could hear my mother's heart breaking. Not a great start in impressing the in-laws, but as Pink so eloquently says, it was time to 'get this party started'.

Bundling back into the Hummers, with sounds of laughter and corks popping, we made our way back to the suite at the MGM for speeches. I'd remembered something my brother had said about wedding speeches years before: if you have to do one you have to refrain from drinking until the 'work' part is over. Well, I was having none of that so I decided to make the speeches as early as possible. It was the best idea ever. They were funny, they were heartfelt and best of all they were finished in record time so we were off downstairs to the private dining room in the fabulous ultra-modern restaurant Fiamma.

During Dan's initial planning enquiries and discussions, the management had suggested we go for a set menu with three choices of starter, main and dessert, but the best suggestion they made was to pay for an hourly package of alcohol. My advice to American restaurants is NEVER challenge Aussies and Brits to an open bar. The night went off like a packet of throw-downs. Everyone was having way too much fun and just when we thought it couldn't get any better, we headed back to the suite for the New Year's Eve fireworks that began their seriously impressive display from the top of every major hotel at midnight all the way up the Strip. They blew for nearly half an hour and all of our guests had a superb view. My brother turned to me halfway through, after listening to the cooing at how amazing the fireworks were, and said, 'This is just a Tuesday night in Sydney.' It was then that I realised, 'I'm married and it's 2006.'

The wedding turned out to be a monumentally wonderful event and I couldn't have asked for anything better. The best part – I was now Dan's wife.

The entire party was still rocking in our room at about 2am when I decided that was enough and pulled up stumps. It was my wedding night and I had no intention of falling into bed too tired to even kiss, so I became an extremely motivated room-clearer! With the whole of Las Vegas as a 'next location' option the gang were more than happy to leave the newlyweds alone as we shut the door on our best day ever.

Recovery lunches are always a blast. The event is over, everyone is relaxed (or hungover) so it's time to sit back, eat and chat about everything that's happened so far. Our recovery lunch was at the Peppermill Fireside Lounge, the swankiest old-school diner in Vegas which truly has to be seen to be believed. Filled with low, cosy booths and anchored at the south end of the room by a fire pit, its flames erupting from a pool of glowing white water, you feel like you have stepped onto the set of *Boogie Nights* and that any minute Dirk Diggler could arrive and shout you a Fluffy Duck. It is hilarious.

Now that all the grown-up stuff was done I could relax and actually listen to our guests' conversation, instead of pasting on that old automatic smile and letting it all wash over me as I had done in the previous few days. I was looking forward to finding out what happened to everyone once they left our room.

Baby Benny, my old flatmate and one of my besties, recounted his favourite tale. Though he and I had met in London I still couldn't believe Benny and I had grown up about three streets away from each other on the Central Coast and yet didn't know each other existed until so many years later. We had been bonded forever after surviving that psycho flatmate. No names, no court cases, but just to give you an idea of exactly how psycho that flatmate was, one night I brought a man I had been seeing home to my place for the first time, for what I prefer to call some overnight romance. The next morning the psycho flatmate bumped into him in the hallway and apparently said, 'Well I hope you used a condom, 'cause if you didn't you'd better get yourself to a clinic . . .'

Can you believe it? The overnight romance stretched on and a few weeks later my paramour told me what had happened. I was furious but also very curious and asked him why he continued dating me. He replied sweetly, 'I thought if you had given me something, as long as it was curable by tablets, I didn't mind as I quite liked you.' What a gentleman.

On the day of the wedding Benny had gone down to meet Juzzy at the grand buffet at the MGM and they were seated at a long mixed table next to three quite obese women. They seemed like a lovely group, Benny said, and were having a giggle with him. When the waitress came over they each ordered the jumbo-sized Diet Coke (about two litres in a plastic mug) and when their drinks arrived at the table, all three of them added a couple of packets of low-joule sweeteners to the already artificially sweetened liquid . . . how good is that? Only in America.

Another classic story came from my official man-maid, Juzzy, about his flight from LA to Vegas. It was supposed to be a 50-minute flight but due to a strong tailwind it was only going to take 45 minutes. When everyone was seated the pilot made an announcement that owing to the now shortened flight, and due to US aviation law, no trolley service would be available, so anyone needing a snack was welcome to grab an $8 voucher from the flight attendant, get off the plane and go and secure some chips or maybe a thickshake before take-off. Nearly EVERYONE got off, which meant a 40-minute delay before they were able to take off. Again, surely, only in America.

After all the stories there were hugs and tears of goodbye as the wedding party headed off in different directions. Some went to Miami for a holiday; some ventured up into Yosemite National Park to party with some grizzlies; others decided to hit the Grand Canyon (not literally!) and Dan and I flew to Cabo San Lucas, on the southernmost tip of the Baja California peninsula in western Mexico, for our honeymoon.

Before the wedding, while I'd been on tour in Ireland, Dan had studied honeymoon options on the internet for weeks before locking in the Pueblo Bonito Pacifica Holistic Retreat and Spa for our first trip as Mr and Mrs. A brand-new, oceanfront boutique hotel on a rugged three-kilometre stretch of beach on the Pacific side of Cabo, it offered every luxury that any normal honeymooner would desire. It was a gem . . . but all we wanted to do when we got there was sleep.

Soon after we'd said our goodbyes in Vegas, Dan had started to feel iffy and then for the first two days of our official honeymoon he had his turn at being super sick with the type of flu that always seems to strike the minute you try to wind down. By the third day he was well enough to leave our room and even though it was quite overcast we decided to relax by the pool. Now normally I am a huge fan of hotel retail therapy but not when it is a complete rip-off. When I found out the cost of a small tube of sunscreen I was stunned. There was no way I was paying the ludicrous amount of money they were asking so I convinced Dan we should wait until we ventured into town the next day and buy some there. It wasn't like the sun was pelting down!

Ever heard the classic statement, 'But we were only out in the sun for an hour . . .'? I've laughed scornfully at that pitiful excuse in the past but now I know it's the truth. Dan and I had no idea we were as badly scorched as we were, though I do recall climbing into the big spa by the pool and commenting that we would have to ask the staff to turn down the thermostat as the water was just silly hot. I thought it strange that nobody else in the pool seemed bothered by it, but it wasn't until we returned to our room that we realised we had cooked ourselves to a nuclear sunburnt red.

Sunstroke is a strange ailment. It all became clear at dinner when, after only one margarita and before ordering our meal, I got up from the table and went to dance (alone) in front of the three-piece mariachi band playing beside the salad bar. Dan told me later he was looking at me, thinking, 'What the hell is she doing?', but he was too sore to move and find out.

As the theme song for *The Love Boat* proclaims, 'love, exciting and new' . . . well our supposedly loved-up honeymoon was neither exciting nor new. We were so ill, sunburnt and heat-affected that we had to stay in the cool dark shade and away from even a hint of the sun's rays. Dan was so burnt that he bled. Our fried condition left us with no choice but to stay in our room. Worse things on a honeymoon you say? Here is the clincher, though: we were both so red-raw, like a freshly scrubbed Karen Silkwood after the radiation spill, that we were unable to touch each other for the remainder of the holiday. Very romantic.

At the end of the honeymoon our burns finally subsided. We returned to LA for a few days before going our separate ways. Dan was heading back to London to work and I was off to New York to start work on the ideas development deal with Picture This TV. It is not ideal for newlyweds to be in different countries for the first month of their marriage, but opportunity is not a lengthy visitor when you are in showbiz so we both knew it had to be.

Juzzy had asked me years before if the soles of my feet were sore from landing on them all the time . . . I didn't think he had a point then but this time I knew I had hit the jackpot: here I was, newly married to the man of my dreams and about to start on the gig of the century.

I was staying with my mate Jena, a Manhattan-based Texan, whom I'd met years before at a barbecue in Oxford and we'd immediately hit it off. She was seeing a British guy, who, like most of the people at the party, was lovely but very jolly-hockey-sticks-oh-I-say-marvellous English, so when we heard each other's accents we were drawn to each other and it didn't take long for me to know she needed to be in my life.

Jena is the sort of girl I want to be when I grow up. She is together, fabulous, hilarious, super intelligent, beautifully groomed, glamorously dressed and über charming with a depth of wisdom that I will more than likely be searching a lifetime for. We talked for hours at that first barbecue and swapped numbers with the intention of catching up. True to our word, we did so when either of us were in each other's city – she even came to Vegas for the wedding. So when I told her I was coming to New York straight after the honeymoon, she insisted I stay in her seriously casual-groovy-chic loft apartment right on Union Square between Greenwich and the East Village.

Well, I thought I was Mary Tyler Moore, throwing my beret in the air while walking up 5th Avenue each day to get to the office, which was just off 42nd Street near Times Square. The whole time I was there I would vary my walk home to get a better understanding of the New York grid and I'd end up surprising myself as I accidentally stumbled across landmarks like Madison Square Garden, the Empire State Building and Grand Central Station. Each time I'd see one, my heart would start racing and even though it's a bit 'Heidi hits the big city', I would shake my head and think, I'm just a girl from Gosford. I live in London and I am working in New York . . . is this a dream? How did I get to be in Whole Foods grabbing urban organic groceries on Park Avenue instead of nicking a few musk sticks from the Springfield shops? It felt amazing.

And the work itself was the most fun ever. Each day I'd turn up at the office to throw around ideas, come up with show concepts and create characters. I have discovered that the television industry in Australia is not really different to that in other countries. Pretty much everywhere, the only way to get a show up is to either be very hot (and not the sunburnt kind) or just the right mix of new. One of the big problems is that it's so hard to be original when you pitch a show idea to the networks. You can virtually guarantee that whatever you do, someone has pitched the parallel idea the day before!

It happened in one of my meetings at the Rockefeller Center. I was with Bryan from Picture This and we had just finished explaining my brilliant show idea when the executive interrupted and said, 'Do you know Adam Hills? He was in here yesterday pitching a similar show.'

Adam is probably best known as the host of the hit ABC show *Spicks and Specks* and I had known him for years. He had compered my first stand-up gig just over 16 years before so it was an amazing coincidence to hear that we were still treading the same boards all these years later. And hilarious that we'd had the same show idea independently.

While I was in New York I helped write the best part of two sitcoms, created two game show ideas and pitched a chat show but, like anything in the entertainment industry, nothing happens quickly. Especially overnight success. I was okay with playing the waiting game but even with the benefit of iChat I was desperately missing Dan. I managed to fill in some of my non-work time in great restaurants and I did become quite the bargain stalker in the shops of Soho but it wasn't enough to keep my mind off what I was missing. After a month I'd had enough of being Mary Tyler Moore and made tracks back home to my hubby.

8

Everybody Needs Good Neighbours

Once we got back to London Dan and I settled easily into married life. It was really no different to the previous couple of years, besides getting used to calling each other 'husband' or 'wife', which made me laugh every time we did. Life had been so hectic that it felt like there was barely enough time to get a load of washing on before it was time to pack up again to fly home to see the family, then kick off a month-long Aussie tour. But this time I was smart and Dan came with me.

Starting in Sydney, the tour finished in Brisbane and I had fun making that fabulous film taster along the way. You already know that was when I noticed my expanding breasts and dashed to the chemist, then the magic stick announced I was pregnant again. Once the shock subsided Dan and I knew there was nothing we could do but hope that this time things would work out. After the ectopic disaster and my mid-air miscarriage we were still not convinced this pregnancy would last, but you know what life's like, we needed to make plans in case it did.

At the end of April 2006 we both flew back to London completely exhausted. Other people in the same situation might settle down, start preparing the baby's room and plod along until the birth but we didn't do that. We decided that with a baby on the way we should get organised, so we came up with the idea of putting our (well, Dan's) flat on the market. Brilliant idea. We could pay off our debts (living in London even with two incomes is all about debt), rid ourselves of a big mortgage and be 'Nil-ionaires' by the time the baby was due. What isn't sensible about that? All we had to do was spruce the old girl up (the flat, not me), find an agent, a buyer and it would be a done deal.

Many flats in London are on what are called 'council estates'. During the Blitz in World War II, London was bombed for 57 consecutive nights and more than a million houses were destroyed. Can you imagine what that must have been like? I can't get my head around it at all. It must have been terrifying. I won't bore you with a whole anti-war diatribe but I found these statistics that put life for most modern middle-class Australians into perspective: more than 43 000 civilians were killed during the Blitz and just on a million civilians were injured on those 57 nights and a series of other mini blitzes that continued throughout the war all over the country. Let me put it this way, what were you complaining about yesterday? The traffic? Your diminished superannuation? Feeling overweight? Now while these are all valid and relative complaints, try feeling that way plus being in a bomb-raid shelter every night (if you were lucky) for almost two months? It's just way too much for my tiny mind.

As a result of all that bombing, the government had to get loads of housing built for the survivors as quickly as possible. And the answer was to build scores of blocks of council estate flats. Many years later, when Margaret Thatcher was Prime Monster, she oversaw a law that allowed council tenants to buy their flats for an extremely reduced rate. The savvy ones then sold them on for the full market value, turning over quite a substantial instant profit. Good for them. It was a great chance to change your financial status and perhaps use the money to move a little further out of London into a much bigger place, which is what so many of them did. The outcome of all that in today's London means that in any estate you will find some of the flats in each block still occupied by council tenants, who are mostly much lower income families, and other flats owned by working people like Dan.

It is a hard situation to describe while trying to be egalitarian, but the council flats (rightly) go to just about anyone on any sort of pension, so once the council rent you one of their flats, for, like, 20 bucks a week, they can't take it back, not even if your situation changes and you end up earning a million pounds a day.

The only residents who end up paying anything extra towards the upkeep of the building, aside from the local taxpayers, are the independent owners. At our place, every other week there seemed to be a bill for £10 000 for our share of the yearly cost of the leaf blowing (I'm not joking), £15 000 for hedge trimming, whatever thousand pounds for a new footpath and so it went on. Our council taxes were already paying for all of the other occupants of the building so we were getting slugged two times over. It was definitely time to sell.

As part of our 'let's get organised for our baby' focus, Dan and I tried to pick up every bit of work we could to save enough money to tide us over when I stopped work. I wanted to do as little stand-up as possible while I was pregnant. Sadly, restricting my work options meant it wasn't our bank account that was growing; the only thing that was gaining was the weight on my behind and it was not a good look.

Just when I was about to convert Dan to a tuna and Ryvita diet, BBC Radio 2 bought a sketch show that had us covered for quite a few months. The show was called *The Powder Room* and was devised, written and performed with two goddesses/phenomenally funny stand-ups. The first was the deliciously naughty English comic actor and writer Lucy Porter, and the second was the urban funk factor that is Nigerian cockney Gina Yashere (any woman who gets to co-host the MOBO [music with black origins] Awards with Coolio is about as urban funk factor as it gets). Oh, and me.

I am not sure if it was the endless supply of Marks & Spencer flapjacks or the chocolate muffins that brought out the best in our writing sessions, but we all had way too many good times for what was meant to be a working environment. Nothing was sacred as we cut a swathe through the general perceptions of what female comics have to offer. We managed to create a riotous spin on everything from weight to skin colour, nationality, height, age, wages, death and, of course, men.

We recorded in front of a live audience in the hallowed ground that is the theatre at RADA (Royal Academy of Dramatic Art). The show was a mixture of sketches and monologues and, as we were all well-seasoned stand-ups, there was plenty of audience interaction too. It was the first all-female sketch show ever to go to air on Radio 2 so we were extremely proud of it. (It did help having Frank 'the Master' Stirling as our producer and the general target of our sexual harassment, which he seemed to take with style and grace.)

Radio is a much bigger deal in the UK than it is in Australia. Breakfast shows are just as important to the British networks as they are in Australia, but in the UK they seem to commission actual shows, not just hire hosts. Like the wireless days of old, this allows many more sitcoms and sketch shows to test their mettle before they hit TV screens. Shows like *Little Britain* and *The League of Gentlemen* got their start on radio.

Many British people will turn the television off (day or evening) to listen to a high-quality radio show and these shows contribute to nearly as many 'water cooler' moments as the telly does. If you think that sounds cool, go to the BBC radio website and click on Radio 2 or 4 and you will find hundreds to choose from.

I guarantee you will laugh listening to comedy programs like *Just a Minute* and *Sorry, I Haven't a Clue*. It is a win/win situation. You'll feel better, because it is scientifically proven that laughter lowers blood pressure, reduces stress and boosts your immune system as well as releasing endorphins (the body's natural painkillers), giving you an improved sense of wellbeing. And you will feel really intelligent for doing so!

I finished *The Powder Room* just in time to head north to my eighth Edinburgh Festival. I was not doing the whole four-week run, just a couple of shows here and there, as well as shooting a role the English comedian Lee Mack had written for me in his BBC sitcom, *Not Going Out*. The rest of the time I was Dan's entourage – it was his year to shine as he opened his first ever Edinburgh show.

One of my closest friends, Jill (who Dan calls his Scottish wife), was kind enough to ask us to stay with her in her flat for the entire time we were in Edinburgh. I'd met Jill when she was doing her show in Edinburgh called 'Will Anne Frank Please Come to the Diary Room'. Without doubt the funniest woman on the planet, Jill makes me do that laugh that sounds like a cross between a hoik and a bark. Spending the month with her was going to be way too much fun.

Dan and I also leapt at the offer because it meant we didn't have to take a chunk out of our savings, the only negative being the 'cement' futon we had to sleep on. Jill's futon mattress may very well have given her the posture of a sentry but I needed a crane to pull me up off the damn thing each day.

I had started to whinge about the many downsides of being pregnant (you'd think I'd just be happy I was still pregnant at all), but while whingeing I made a startling discovery. When you are pregnant you get to whinge and moan all the time and loved ones listen without interjecting with smarty-arse comments. It is glorious.

That year the Festival was not the usual wild time for me, for obvious reasons, but I was happy to keep a much lower profile. The changes my body was going through were making me feel less than my usual sparkly self and Dan and I were both feeling anxious about our flat. We'd had it on the market for nearly five months and there'd been no offers. We knew we had to go home and put our grown-up ducks all in a line.

Coming back to London, I looked at everything with a fresh eye. Summer was coming to an end and the leaves were starting to fall all around our area. The colour of the trees was just starting to change to those sweet yellow autumnal tones and the flat was looking its flirty best. It was the perfect time to accentuate the positives and revamp our sales efforts.

If I followed any self-respecting real estate agent's lead I would give would-be buyers the following spiel:

A gorgeous flat overlooking the lush greenery of one of Highgate's stunning tree-lined and quiet streets, just a whisper from the gates of Hampstead Heath. All three double bedrooms are light and airy with superbly high ceilings that frame tall windows flanked by billowing Egyptian cotton white curtains. The spacious yet intimate loungeroom is complemented by a projector screen TV on the west wall and an impressively well appointed kitchen with large windows overlooking a generously large backyard.

But with any real estate pitch we know all is not as it seems. Yes, the street was tree-lined and impressive but our flat was actually on a sort of three-way little bitumen roundabout, which was home to a phone box that was systematically vandalised every time the phone company replaced the glass. In the daytime, our street was reasonably quiet, however, at night the area came to life (and not in a good way), with the phone-box-roundabout playing host to various drug deals, domestic bust-ups and loud abusive phone calls. It was all very relaxing.

One night Dan and I were on the lounge catching an episode of *The West Wing* when we noticed a red spinning light going around the room, from what we concluded could only be a fire engine. I am the biggest Mrs Busybody when I am at home, so I slid up to the window, making sure I kept just out of sight, and saw three fire engines parked outside.

Not being able to help myself, I grabbed the keys and headed down onto the street in my jarmies, with a pashmina stylishly thrown around my shoulders. There is something about a man in a full fireman's outfit that makes me go all giddy. It must be their big hoses. *Grrr.*

It turned out they were evacuating the building next door because apparently one of the flats was a crack den which had been petrol-bombed by some dissatisfied former customers. Yikes. Well, I stayed out the front for about an hour passing on the crack den information to anyone who wanted to listen. I thought it was very civic-minded of me, and by contrast it made our block of flats seem like 'Walton Mountain'. Mind you, let he who is without flat issues cast the first petrol bomb.

Our building was not *too* bad. There were eight flats in total, with two on each floor. And the inhabitants were quite an eclectic mix. This is how I summed us all up:

Number 1: A very agreeable chap in his late 50s who was at work every day and kept to himself after hours.

Number 2: A sweet and thoughtful Greek Cypriot widow who was a passionate gardener and kept her garden in almost Chelsea-Flower-Show shape.

Number 3: A young, nice single mum with two little boys, one a baby and the other the loudest five-year-old in the whole wide world. They also had two cats, two dogs, a ferret and two birds, all in a flat no bigger than an average loungeroom.

Number 4: A stylish young couple who emanated fabulosity . . . okay, too much, I know. Yes, this was us.

Number 5: Another single mum but a much more motivated and groovy woman who was into composting and taking courses at the community centre while working part time. Her son was very well mannered and about nine.

Number 6: Another single mum, a cool Jamaican social worker with dreadlocks whose fragrance was a heady mixture of ylang ylang and weed. Her son, who was about 18 years old, was an aspiring rap artist whom Dan and I nicknamed the 'Bedroom Gangster'. We could never tell if he was rapping or abusing his girlfriend since the only word we could ever clearly decipher was 'FOKK'.

Number 7: A single guy in his early 40s who rode a bike and kept an extremely low profile.

And then there was Number 8. Occupying Number 8 was a woman in her early 50s, maybe even late 40s, but it was impossible to tell as she was a binge-drinking smack addict with multiple mental health issues. She would constantly spend time in a facility only to return a few weeks later, clean and ready to start again. Her son was a 17-year-old goth who would go missing for days on end – we guessed to get away from his mother.

All in all, not too bad. London isn't really a 'get to know your neighbours' kind of town, so even living side by side like we did for nearly four years this was all I knew about our fellow dwellers – until we went to sell up. Then it was on for young and old.

Because we hadn't had any takers we dropped our selling price to see if that would help. It did, and brought a whole new world of interested buyers our way.

Now a word of hard-earned advice: Never stay at home when you are pregnant and potential buyers are going through your house. In the UK, showing the house yourself is part of the selling process so I had to do it quite often and it wasn't pretty. Sure, I might have been a little moody with the super-strength pregnancy hormones messing me up and perhaps the added stress of having to do the face-to-face selling didn't help, but overhearing the morons commenting on how small our storage space was made me feel like banging their heads together and locking them in the so-called teeny-tiny space. 'Plenty of room in there now, ay suckers?' Who knew when I greeted them with polite small-talk and the smell of percolating coffee and chocolate chip cookies fresh out of the oven that it would turn so nasty?

There were a few sound issues in our building but so far, thanks to good timing, the potential buyers had not been exposed to them. I did mention the loudest boy in the whole wide world who lived across the hall. Billy was a sweet little boy but he only had one volume. Whether he was happy or sad, excited or angry, he was always turned up to eleven. His bedroom was right next to ours and the walls were made out of Japanese rice paper, so when he got up in the morning it was very much a case of one up, all up. Billy liked to bounce a soccer ball against our wall from about 6am but by this time we were already awake and seething because prior to his wall-soccer practice he would let his cats and dogs out of his flat but not out of the building. The resulting early-morning chorus of meows and woofs funnelled up the stairwell with the acoustics of an abandoned hospital and woke Dan and I with a start. EVERY MORNING!

It's harsh to blame every interrupted sleep-in on Billy, as the Bedroom Gangster upstairs did his fair share of messing with our REM sleep. He would invite several of his 'homies' around to have some beers and a few 'j's in the backyard and then they'd be fired up and ready to go upstairs and make some music, man. ('Mother mother fokk, getta cop 'n' lock a fokk, mun', or words to that effect are etched into my brain for all time.) And if that wasn't enough, every couple of days he and his girlfriend would have an almighty row. The girlfriend had the best look, which in London is called the 'Croydon Facelift'. You pull your high ponytail so tightly on top of your head that it actually pulls up the skin on your face. Her little Pekinese dog, Cartier (with a silent 't', pronounced kar-ee-air), wore the same look. Whenever she used to scream her pooch's name in the corridor, I always wondered if a yappy dog's name was what Louis-François Cartier had in mind when he launched his opulent brand in the mid-19th century. Mmm. Yes, I know I sound awfully snobby when I describe the other residents, but if you are in London and an Australian is the poshest person in the building, then there are issues.

But no one in the building caused us as much grief as the woman living in the top-floor flat, Number 8. She was the full fruit and nut bar. Now I am not making light of poor mental health, nor am I judging a person's drug and alcohol addiction, but when this affects your daily life in a residential capacity it is hard not to be a little grumpy. Add pregnancy and trying to sell your home on top of that and you have one cranky Australian.

I had realised Veruka was a worry very early on and kept my distance. The fact that she lifted the internal letterbox flap on our front door and called to us asking for a spare fag was a dead giveaway that all was not right. I was in the kitchen and nearly had a heart attack. A few weeks later she knocked on our door and told Dan her son had locked her out so could she wait in our loungeroom until the fire brigade came to bash her door down. They arrived two hours later. We were very polite but didn't enter into too many chats with her after that.

And you didn't need to be street-wise to realise that there was a bit more going on than just booze. In the middle of the night we would be woken by screaming drug dealers banging on the door downstairs yelling things like, 'You've got your stuff now where is my f£$@%^& money, Veruka, I am going to fu%*^% kill you . . .' Very relaxing.

Another time she came to the door and accused Dan of stealing her life story. She gave him a really old floppy disk and said, 'That is the real story, Mr Writer, not your story which you have stolen from me.' Dan just said, 'Okay, thank you, I am going to close the door now' as he gave her back her disk of craziness.

As if all that wasn't enough, every few months she would go right off the deep end and have a stand-off with the police, throwing all sorts of things at them from her top-floor windows. The police would then call the fire brigade to bash down her door and then the ambulance to take her to the local mental health ward at a nearby hospital.

And we were surprised the flat wasn't selling?

But it wasn't just the people living in our building who made noise. The council were also responsible for their fair share. Every day they liked to provide a different 'service' that began just as Billy was kicking the soccer ball. The leaf blowing starting at 6am was a highlight, as it was completed while it was actually too dark to see any of the leaves. Emptying the recycling bottle bank was another personal favourite, along with the garbos who stopped for their early-morning smoko, leaving their trucks idling for 30 minutes in the process. However, all of those noises paled into insignificance when the jackhammers arrived to pull up the perfectly functioning footpath to make way for the individually 'cut outside my door' cement tiles.

Most of the 500-metre stretch of our street had been done many months before, but the part outside our building had been left untouched – we had hoped it might be finished while we were in Edinburgh, but who were we kidding? You can imagine how pleased we were, after a nice long summer break, that the council was ready to resume work – of course, at the same time as the real estate's sales team went into action mode to sell our flat.

Then it happened. The most delightful couple, who reminded us of how we were when we first met, came to look at our flat. Walking around, they just seemed to grow more and more excited about the place. It was in their price range, it wasn't too big and they were in love with the area and had wanted to live there for a long time. I felt a small twinge of guilt that I wasn't filling them in about the ongoing problems but I knew I couldn't. This was real estate and everyone knows that there is always something you don't know about the place you buy. And who knows, maybe Veruka would stay clean, Billy would become obsessed with knitting and the rapper would take a vow of silence. These things *can* happen! It looked like we might just have a sale and we were so excited . . . but that excitement was short-lived. And it was all our fault.

We had been woken in the middle of the night by Veruka (yet again) screeching from her flat and we looked out the window to see two police cars and a fire truck. She was throwing big paint tins, plates, knives, pots, pans, mattresses, clothes and basically anything she could get her hands on at them. Dan and I had had enough, but what can you do? She was a council tenant so she would never be evicted. We were hostages to her behaviour and the sale of our flat hung in the balance every time she had a drink or took drugs. It just felt so unfair.

So the next morning, after Dan cleaned up the entire garden, we wrote an official letter of complaint to the council, complete with a time-line of the years of harassment. We sent it off and felt marginally better. Well, we did until we spoke to the real estate agent later that morning.

The good news was that the sweet couple had made an offer and wanted to know if they could come over that evening for a second viewing, so they could take some measurements for their furniture, etc. We knew Veruka had been taken away and was now receiving good medical care for what was usually at least a few weeks, so we were fine with that.

When we told the real estate about the letter, we got the bad news. Because we had lodged an official complaint, by law this had to be disclosed in any contracts relating to the sale of the property. Can you believe it? We'd written the letter and sent it off not even three hours before. Could we not have waited? I seriously could have punched myself.

At 4pm there was a knock at our door. Before I tell you who it was, just remember at that point I was eight months pregnant and what seemed like the make or break of our financial future was now wrapped up in the selling of this cursed flat.

I opened the door and it was VERUKA. Her eyes were like saucers and she stank of booze and joints. She stank so badly of joints, in fact, that getting a waft of her made me feel like I needed a Tim Tam. Now I am going to paraphrase her exact words but they went something along the lines of: 'I know what you did and I know that you picked up all my stuff from the garden and I want it back.' I closed the door on her mid-sentence which may seem harsh but I was paranoid she would do something to me and I was in no state to fight back. When you are unsure of someone's measure and you are eight months knocked up, it is best to err on the side of caution.

When I rang Dan and told him 'she' was back he let out a frustrated sigh of defeat. Sometimes things spiral so far out of control that you just have to accept your inevitable downfall.

By 6pm, when Dan got home, Veruka had stormed out of the building and hadn't come back. Oh my God, could we be that lucky? Hopefully she would follow her usual pattern and stay on a bender, not returning until late evening. So we steeled ourselves and set about creating the perfect atmosphere.

The lighting was warm and chic, the music was some 'how smug are we' Sarah Vaughan and it was a quiet, balmy evening. Dan had decided we should open a bottle of wine for our buyers but not encourage them to stay too long. We were all set.

At 7pm the intercom buzzed and I answered it excitedly.

'Ah yes, good evening, sorry to disturb, this is the Kentish Town Police. Can we come up and have a word with you?'

I think I said, 'You cannot be serious.' So up they came and I was stunned with disbelief.

'We have had a complaint from the neighbour in Number 8 that you have stolen some of her things . . .'

I interrupted him and blurted out just some of the history – her drug taking, the constant arrests, the fire brigade, the sale of our flat and how every time it looked like we were closing in on a buyer she would spin out and the whole thing would go awry. I told him about our impending financial implosion and how there was another potential buyer due to arrive in the next 30 minutes so I was not the slightest bit surprised that she had gone off the deep end yet again. I made it very clear that if he wanted to locate any of the things from the front garden that morning then it was best to go out to the big bins at the back and start searching. He was a nice cop and started to sympathise with me, but it was all too late – I was screeching through gritted teeth like I was possessed as I pointed out that if she didn't get the f@$% away from the building in the next half an hour I was going to kill her myself. (Always good to tell a police officer you want to kill someone.)

He could tell I was at the end of my proverbial tether (whatever that means!) and promised me that they would do their best to keep Veruka away from the building for the next couple of hours. Then he wished us all the best as he escaped from our flat as quickly as possible.

At 7.30pm the intercom buzzed again but this time it was our buyers, so we floated to the door like Margo and Jerry in *The Good Life*.

Various 'hellos' and 'lovely-to-see-yous' ensued as we cracked open a bottle of South African sauvignon and bid each other good health. We told them to go and have another good look around while Dan and I stayed in the loungeroom and made faces at each other like a couple of scaredy cats. All seemed well and I started to relax a little.

Dan and the husband got down to the business of bills and room measurements while the wife and I talked babies and how long we had both been married. We then drifted into the back bedroom to continue our chats. With all four of us having quite a social time I dashed back into the lounge for my glass of water as I didn't want to be the only one not holding a glass.

Reflected red, blue and white lights were now strobing our loungeroom. My heart sank as I peered out of the front window. I counted two fire engines, three police cars and an ambulance. Oh, but wait, there's more. In front of the ambulance headlights I could see Veruka in what looked like some kind of Mexican stand-off. I became instantly incandescent with rage but managed to keep a lid on it long enough to call out to Dan and our buyers that I was just ducking downstairs. I didn't wait for a reply and tore out of the flat as fast as my off-balance eight-month-pregnant body would allow me.

By the time I got out the front I was frothing at the mouth. Have you ever launched into a fury-filled rant using a stage whisper? I must have looked like a bigger maniac than Veruka. The police explained to me that there was nothing they could do under the Mental Health Act and it was up to the fire brigade to smash down her door so she could get into her flat. Once she was inside they could get the ambulance to take her away after they made a thorough search of her property. What??!! It made absolutely no sense to me, so I watched in complete astonishment as the firemen filed up the stairs and started to break Veruka's door down.

It was only about five minutes after the crash of the door opening and Veruka starting to yell before our buyers made their way out of the building and past the emergency services circus. Dan was behind them and we both knew it was over as they wished us all the best and disappeared into the night.

The next morning they officially withdrew their offer and we were back to square one. Honestly, I think I am the one who needed some time out in the mental health facility. I could have secured a bed next to Veruka and got some very much needed shut-eye. As I have said to you before . . . what do you do?

We dropped the price again to see how we would get on but by that stage the summer was well and truly over and the market had slowed right down. Maybe it wasn't as dramatic as I thought but in my mind the grim spectre of bankruptcy was edging ever closer, as was the birth of our first child.

Then one perfect day . . . a girl in her early twenties rocked through the door for an inspection. She said her father was going to buy her a flat and he would be using cash, so they were happy for a quick settlement. We were in such low spirits that we decided to adopt a policy of full disclosure. We told her about the Bedroom Gangster and his penchant for rap; we told her about Billy, the loudest boy in the whole wide world; and, of course, we told her about Veruka and her recurring episodes of madness. (Okay, maybe not full disclosure . . . we didn't tell her about the leaf-blower serenade.)

Despite all these tiny problems the fact remained that it was a great flat in a fantastic location so she decided to go for it. Her dad came to have a look and commented that his daughter would probably be louder than all of the building put together so it seemed like a match made in heaven.

I was almost delirious as the papers were signed but we were too paranoid to pack until we exchanged contracts, so we crossed our fingers and hoped I wasn't going to sour another deal by writing something that would come back to bite us. Far from a complaint letter this time, I was actually penning a 15-minute radio play for BBC Radio 4. I had written it about our adventures selling the flat and Dan was absolutely beside himself that the play would air before the property was settled. Of course, with my usual impeccable timing, it did air before the deal was watertight but thankfully the new buyers mustn't have been Radio 4 listeners, so the flat stayed sold. (In the play I killed Veruka, which was incredibly satisfying . . . is that wrong?)

Most people celebrate when they sell their property but Dan and I didn't; we were too battle scarred. We quietly exhaled and thanked our lucky stars that we could finally pack up and move out. And just as we were exiting our old home our baby was scheduled to do the same. But as I have come to learn, babies have their own schedules that have nothing to do with the mother, the doctor, or a visiting grandmother-to-be.

And Ruby Makes Three

'When did we get this much stuff?' I asked Dan exasperatedly as we were packing to move. I had arrived in the UK with one suitcase and couldn't fathom why I was now standing in a rather large loungeroom, cornered by floor-to-ceiling boxes. I am a mad culler and every time I move house (this was the eighth time in eight years), I would throw out anything I hadn't used in a while – clothes, music, videos, DVDs, the lot. Dan was similar, so to think this mountain of stuff was the basics made me feel quite queasy. Maybe the fact that I was burstingly pregnant was adding to my sense of unease.

Packing and third-trimester pregnancy are not great friends. We were moving two weeks before my due date, so instead of nesting and relaxing like my expectant 'sisters', I was wrapping glasses in newspaper and putting the 'nursery' in a crate.

My godsend of a mother had flown over for four weeks to help me with secret women's business like packing the flat to move, then unpacking at the new house and, of course, the most important job of having the kettle ready for when we brought home her first grandchild. Dad was back in Australia keeping the home fires burning and maintaining a close eye on the iChat video phone to find out how we were going.

Dan and I had found a little rental house in a quiet corner (we hoped) of yet another council estate in Woodside Park, two stops from the end of the Northern Line. It was a leafy, incredibly suburban locale, nestled in the armpit of High Barnet, about 40 minutes by train from town. It offered none of the benefits of living in London and none of the benefits of not living in London, but after the continuous dramas of the old flat we were looking forward to living in a calm neighbourhood and this seemed like the place. It reminded me of the Talking Heads song 'Road to Nowhere' and I had my fingers crossed that anyone who'd settled there had left their drug and alcohol addiction, paranoid angst, amplifiers and soccer balls somewhere else.

The main claim to fame for our street (I love that people, me included, always find something to make their suburb special) was the fact that Spike Milligan had lived here. Who would have guessed that Spike and I would both have spent time in Woodside Park *and* Woy Woy (which he once described as the world's only above-ground cemetery)?

I had been living in London for so long that there were aspects of the place I didn't even notice any more. Like, for example, the state of the community centre I had been visiting for all my midwife appointments throughout my pregnancy. When I took Mum there for one of my final check-ups I thought she was going to collapse in shock. Mum had lived in London for a few years when she was in her twenties and had travelled there many times since, so she is well aware of what the city is like, but visiting 'London' and visiting 'urban London' can be like travelling to two different countries.

In the middle of a rough estate in Kentish Town, the community centre was fenced in by lots of barbed wire and plenty of used needles littered its perimeter. It was so grotty and rundown that it conjured up comparisons with the images my mother saw of the Gaza Strip on the TV news (except for the needles), not a community centre in the middle of London. I hadn't batted an eyelid when I first saw the place but I'd been living under siege from Veruka for so long that nothing much shocked me at the time.

The health system in the UK is so stretched with staff shortages and low wages that I never saw the same midwife twice, which made it difficult to build any sort of relationship or have any continuity of care. I am lucky; I am strong, healthy and my pregnancy had no real complications but I would hate to think about the outcome if I had required special attention.

The midwives were of varying nationalities, with different accents and grasps on English. With such a wide a range of religious beliefs, they all gave me conflicting and, at times, confusing advice on how things should be done. None of them liked me to question them and assumed that I'd accept everything they said (even if it was a total contradiction to what I had been told on a previous visit). Unless there is something wrong you don't get to see an obstetrician at all for the whole nine months.

When Mum had booked her trip she'd had loads of trouble securing a return flight. Not only did she have to factor in when the baby might arrive she also had to juggle price and availability because it was so close to Christmas. She finally gambled on heading home on 7 December (two weeks after the due date), hoping that the baby would come out on time. (Why do airlines do that? They double the price of travel at the very times that you are homesick and want to see your family and then complain, 'Oh, we only made about 600 million dollars in profit this year, things have been really tough.' *Grrr*, who do I kill?)

Every day was like a month for those last few weeks. I tried shopping, curry, acupuncture, pinchy nipple work, walking, raspberry leaf tea, blowing up balloons, driving down bumpy roads and even a bit of rolling around, but nothing was working, nothing. (I have concluded that all those options are merely old wives' tales invented to try to keep a pregnant woman busy so they don't go insane waiting.)

With a week till the baby was scheduled to appear, I suggested that Mum go to Ireland to visit our cousins. I was putting my faith in Murphy's Law – that if anything was going to bring this baby on it would be having to get Mum back in the country within hours. I was so ready to not have to go to the toilet every five minutes and to get my centre of gravity back that I was determined to try anything. But this child was refusing to move.

Finally, at 40 weeks I started the long and undignified road to being induced. The midwives thought it best for me to wait and undergo monitoring each day before they would suggest a date. So, okay, maybe a few days and then I would be scheduled for delivery? I could cope with that (just!).

But no.

It wasn't two days, it was two weeks. TWO WEEKS!

Every day I would lumber into the hospital, be strapped to a heart monitor for three or four hours and then I would get a nice little treat in the form of a sweep. Do you know what I mean by 'sweep'? It's a natural form of induction but anyone who's had one will know the horror of exactly what I'm talking about and I won't go into detail for fear of scaring off any woman who intends on having a child or even those who don't want one. Let's just say the name of the procedure is much gentler than the invasion of the action. (*Owwww.*) It was the perfect fortnight and I can't recommend it more highly . . . as something to avoid if humanly possible.

In addition to feeling like I had completely lost all control and ownership of my body, I was feeling more and more guilty that Mum had travelled halfway across the planet to spend time with her newborn grandchild and now she was going to get hardly any time with the baby (if any at all). I know it was no one's fault, just a case of terrible timing, but I still felt guilty.

Finally a date was set and I was asked to attend the hospital for induction on the evening of 5 December. I was exactly 42 weeks to the day.

Can I suggest if you have a weak constitution or if you are pregnant with your first baby, then it might be a good idea to skip the rest of this chapter and move directly to Chapter 10. If, however, you don't fit into those two categories and are up for it then strap yourself in, 'cause we are in for a bumpy ride.

With the baby two weeks late, I have to say that patience was not in my bag of virtues. Every step of the way seemed to take far too long. The midwives started to talk about induction but the late pregnancy hormones had kicked in and my attention span was about two minutes so everything went in one ear and out the other. I thought I knew what to expect once I checked into hospital on the 5th. I was wrong.

I was shown to my ward and informed that someone would be back soon to induce me. I was happy with that because I thought it meant that hopefully by the time morning had broken, Mum would have one whole day to spend with me and my new bub.

The ward was pretty basic. There were five other women in my room, all in different stages of the birthing process. The woman next to me already had her baby by her side; the three opposite my bed were all moaning with early contractions; and the one on the end near the bathroom was, like me, waiting to be induced. She had about seven family members surrounding her bed and every one of them was complaining loudly about the level of care.

I had read everything I could about childbirth when I was pregnant but I had skipped the 'being induced' chapters. They seemed unnecessary at the time. I hadn't even bothered to find out how the induction starts. So Dan and I went about our business unpacking and drawing the curtains so we could have some privacy, only to hear a shocking sound coming from one of the women opposite. It was a combination grunt and scream that morphed into a high-pitched demand . . . '*geeeeeet eeeeeeeer*'.

To say the staff were aggressive would be an understatement. I did appreciate that they were completely overworked and grossly underpaid but when I am in a medical situation I turn into the very sweetest version of myself, so I do expect, at the very least, some sort of smile as a reward for being so easygoing. No such luck.

After about two hours one of the nurses came in and said, 'Sorry, we are too busy tonight, we will give you the induction gel in the morning.'

Quite apart from feeling like my baby was being overcooked I couldn't believe that because of this delay Mum was probably not going to see her grandchild at all. Maybe it was a weird and spoilt thing to bring up but as soon as I finished explaining the situation I could see the nurse was irate. She snapped back at me, saying, 'Well, that is how it is. Your mum has nothing to do with me.'

We had desperately tried to change Mum's flight several times but there were no options; all the pre-Christmas flights were full. The only option was buying her a one-way ticket for £1700 (AU$4350) but that flight wasn't available until late January which meant Mum would have to stay for another eight weeks. The whole thing was a bit of a mess but there was nothing any of us could do about it (and the nurse sure wasn't going to speed things up for us).

All I could do was get into my jarmies and kiss Dan goodbye as he headed home to get some sleep. Hmmmm . . . sleep! There is nothing quite like the relaxation of the maternity ward to interrupt a good night's shut-eye. The newborn next to my bed didn't stop crying but that was low-key compared to the other noises in my ward. I had started to think I was in hospital with Bob Marley's Wailers judging from the grunting and moans haunting the room all night long.

Day broke not a moment too soon and despite the fact I had not been able to sleep it was time to be induced . . . or at least that's what I thought. It was hard to tell what the nurses planned as they spent the majority of the time ignoring me. 'Like sands through an hourglass' the morning stretched on and on, with no one coming near me except Dan. I lay in a sleep-deprived stupor watching the ever-changing landscape of the ward.

By mid-afternoon the crying baby had gone home and two of the women in labour overnight had been sent down to the delivery ward. I had learned my lesson the night before so I had been sweetness and light whenever approached by any staff – I hadn't whinged or moaned about anything, but my power to endure without complaint was now on the wane.

'Could someone please tell me when I will be seen by a doctor?' I begged to one nurse as the day started to evaporate.

'Wait your turn,' came the very curt response.

I was treated like a rowdy kid in line at the school tuckshop, not a 38-year-old VERY pregnant woman asking for some basic information. Finally, at 3pm, a nurse came in and announced, 'Okay, open your legs. I am going to put in the gel.' I guess, like any abusive relationship, you just keep accepting events as they unfold, not noticing how bad things actually are.

I have done quite a bit of reading since that day and the 'gel', a synthetic oxytocin (contraction-inducing hormone), does not always work the first time but let me tell you within about 15 minutes I started to have contractions. Within 30 minutes I was doubled over on the bed, wracked with intense pain. I called for the nurse and she took one look at me writhing in agony and told me that I was not in pain yet, so just relax. Oh . . . so easy!

Dan had a doctor in South London years ago who had been a GP in the slums of Calcutta before coming to the UK. Whenever Dan went in to see him with the flu or an ear or throat infection, the doctor would send him away, saying, 'There is nothing wrong with you, I will not treat you. Go home.'

Dan could only guess at the horrific things this doctor must have seen over the years to give him absolutely no tolerance for 'my nose is blocked and I have a sore throat'. I imagine a similar reason explained why the nurses were reacting to me so harshly. With the National Health Service in such an overextended state, many English nurses had gone abroad for better pay, or were pursuing other areas of private care. Some had even left and gone into entirely different careers altogether, refusing to accept such poor wages and working conditions. This meant the staff in the big London hospitals had been enticed over to the UK from countries like Nigeria, Sudan, Somalia, Ethiopia, Uganda and Jamaica.

When I said I was in a great deal of pain, they were obviously hearing 'I'm experiencing a little twinge of discomfort', and seeing a woman in her fancy pyjamas lucky enough to be in a modern hospital at the start of a perfectly natural process. It is the only explanation I can think of . . . otherwise they were sadists.

Two hours later the intensity of my contractions had not changed. I was scared and kept thinking, 'If it gets any worse I am going to explode.' By this stage Mum arrived to join Dan at my bedside for moral support but she found me in agony and unable to communicate at all except through a series of animalistic grunts. Still the nurses wouldn't even throw me a Panadol. Again they argued, 'That is not pain, it is going to get much worse before you need any medication.'

Knowing the healing powers of a cuppa, Mum went off to make us all some tea. There was a room opposite our ward marked by a sign that said 'Maternity refreshments, please wash up after you'. Halfway through dangling a teabag in a cup, a nurse came in and screamed at Mum, 'Get out of here, this is not the damn Hyatt.'

For a supposedly top London hospital with an excellent reputation, it all just beggared belief.

By 8pm my pain was still insane so one of the nurses finally gave me a couple of Panadol. As if that would help! I had been doing all of the right things like taking a walk around the floor, resting for contractions and the only medical attention I received was every hour or so when one of the nurses came to give me yet another sweep. I was starting to feel like a hand puppet.

I was struggling to tell Mum and Dan that the pain was as intense as it had been at 3.30 that afternoon when the curtain to my little private Idaho swung open and in walked the woman who'd been admitted to the next bed earlier that day.

'Ay, I thought I heard an Aussie accent. I'm an Aussie too, how ya garn?'

I was gravely mistaken when I thought my pain could not get worse.

Sharonda, as it turned out, hailed from about 100 kilometres south of Mt Isa but fate had brought her to the end of my bed. She had been listening to our conversations for most of the afternoon and felt that this was the right moment to introduce herself.

'My boyfriend, Trevor, is still at work and I'm not being induced till tomorra so when I heard that youse were Aussies, then I thought I would make m'self known.'

'Please tell me this is not happening' was the only thought that kept running around in my head when Sharonda said, in a tone that suggested that she may have cracked the Da Vinci Code, 'Hey, I know who you used to be!'

If you kill yourself during labour is that considered to be suicide or self-defence?

I was horrified when Sharonda perched herself on the end of my bed and kept talking about where she knew me from. And Dan answered her!

Dan: 'Was it from *Full Frontal*?'

Sharonda: 'Nah, I never watched *Full Frontal*, what was it?'

Dan: 'Was it *In Melbourne Tonight*?'

Sharonda: 'Nah, we never got that up north, God, what was it?'

Then Mum helped out with: 'Maybe it was *Beauty and the Beast* with Stan?'

Sharonda: 'Nah, wasn't that 'cause I never watched him.'

I was now unsure if my guttural groaning was a result of my labour pains or having to listen to this unbearable conversation.

Are you the type of person who goes out of your way to be nice to people who clearly have no regard for you or your privacy and the way you might be feeling? I am so like that and I don't just do it every now and then, I am a repeat offender. So is Dan and so is Mum, so it wasn't until Sharonda said, 'Oh well, I'll think of it. Hey, how black are the nurses? I haven't even seen a white staff member yet. I feel like I'm at a hospital in the Congo . . .' that it was time to either have her killed or ask her to go back to her own bed. The appropriate awkward moments followed, the curtains parted and we were thankfully alone again.

By 10pm the nurses finally believed I was in a bit of pain when I started screaming 'EPIDURAL, EPIDURAL, EPIDURAL' at the top of my huskily labour-diminished voice.

They snapped into action and transferred me to a wheelchair with no rubber on the tyres which looked like it might have been made at the turn of the previous century. I was wheeled stutteringly into the lift but not before the doors closed on one of my legs.

I hope you don't think I'm embellishing any of this story for effect. Even as I am typing I'm still in a world of disbelief while reliving the shock.

Once I got to the birthing room things started to improve, as the nurses actually answered me without snarling. Then, about 45 minutes after I arrived there, the most heavenly anaesthetist turned up and said, 'I can give you an epidural as long as we don't have to talk about the cricket.' The Brits had been losing to the Aussies so he didn't want to hear it!

Who had been keeping me from the epidural? Oh my goodness, I moved instantly into a different world. A world where the staff were civil, a world where I could breathe, in fact, the epidural was so fantastic that I reckon I could have hopped off the bed and hosted a dinner party.

The difference was unimaginable. I'd been at the same level of pain intensity for eight long, slow hours and then . . . nothing. I wished at that moment I was just a little bit religious so I had some higher power to give thanks to but the cricket-loving anaesthetist was God enough.

Two more hours passed by with ease but my cervix was still not dilating, so some sort of hormonal drip was put into my hand while I continued ploughing through an *OK* magazine. It was now in the early hours of the morning and the fact that Mum only had four and a half hours left before she had to leave for Heathrow Airport was playing heavily on all of our hearts. There was nothing we could do.

We hadn't expected the nightmare labour to go on so long. Mum had arrived at the hospital without packing her bags, so I sent her and Dan home to prepare for the flight. The doctors were sure nothing would happen in the hour they would be away, so it seemed to make sense.

Wouldn't you know it, they were only gone about 20 minutes before a series of alarms started going off inside and outside the room. The staff came running through the door like I was in an episode of *ER*. I didn't know what was happening until someone said the baby's heartbeat was starting to plummet. I knew it was bad because for the first time since checking into the hospital 30 hours earlier I was examined by an obstetrician. (Actually, it was the first time in the entire pregnancy.)

The obstetrician didn't say one word to me or look me in the eye. I was scared and alone and my baby was in danger and he couldn't even raise an eyeball to me. Where were the Mark Greene or John Carter-style doctors? They can't only exist in television shows?

The alarms stopped and the tension in the room dissolved as the staff stabilised the baby, then everyone left the room as quickly and as mysteriously as they had come. The midwife stayed behind to tell me that the baby was in a bit of distress but it was still too soon to make decisions.

Decisions? What decisions? Why didn't they just cut the baby out? I had no real information, I was frustrated, frightened and very teary. Mum and Dan seemed to be taking forever, so when they walked back through the door my relief could not stem the flood of my tears.

Another hour passed excruciatingly by and I was a complete basketcase, almost afraid to move in case it hurt the baby somehow. I was trying not to cry and to keep calm but I could feel panic rising.

Beep, beep, beep, beep, beep . . . the alarm went off again and seconds later there was another *ER* bust-in. This time the doctor ordered Dan to dress in full scrubs (he still didn't talk to me) and I was wheeled off to theatre, leaving Mum behind in the room by herself not knowing what the hell was going on.

Literally as he held his scalpel to my skin poised to cut an emergency C-section, the doctor suddenly screamed, 'She's fully dilated, okay, push, push, push.'

I was thinking, 'Are they all on drugs? What do they mean push?' I could not feel anything in the surrounding regions, so how was I to know if I was pushing or not? And who the hell is vacuuming at this time of night? All I could think about was Mum, left by herself, and how terrified she must have been feeling.

Then, at 3.57am, without much fuss (*not much!*) Ruby Charlotte made her first celebrity guest appearance on my tummy. She was sticking her tongue in and out and making Dan and I laugh (well, cry/laugh). I just couldn't believe she was finally out and alive.

Dan ran off to tell Mum that everything was okay and when he returned he took Ruby to be weighed. I don't really remember the rest of the 'housekeeping' but it was not long before I was being wheeled back into the recovery room where Mum, Dan and Ruby were anxiously waiting.

'Well, that wasn't so hard was it?' I said as all three of us (Ruby stayed quiet) commenced our group bawl. The midwife popped her head in to make sure we were all okay and calmly told us the baby was lucky to survive. She then warned me to be careful with all of my stitches (what stitches?) and then said her goodbyes, as her shift was about to end. She also told me not to worry as another nurse would be along shortly to talk me through feeding and recovery.

The hour or so Mum had with Ruby seemed to fly by. She handed Dan her granddaughter, we hugged and then it was time for her to leave. My mum is a legend. How much can one woman take? Not just being away from my dad for four weeks or being in the hospital for what was one of the most distressing nights of her life but she then had to step onto a plane for 24 hours. She is made of seriously strong stuff.

I made Dan go home after dropping Mum at the airport as I could see he was moving into zombie mode. I'd been told I'd just be slipping in and out of sleepy town all day with Ruby, so it didn't seem a drama. By this stage I was so exhausted from the prolonged labour and completely emotionally spent. If I'd had the energy I would have cried for hours but I could barely find the strength to breathe, so dealing with the feelings bubbling below my surface calm would have to wait.

Once they'd gone I waited for the nurse to appear and all of a sudden it was time to move me back up to the 'nightmare on ward street'. It was an equally pleasant journey going back upstairs as it had been going down but at least now I had a baby to show for it. Thank sweet Jesus. When I arrived it seemed I had the entire ward to myself, for the time being anyway.

I asked for my curtain to be drawn as my new bed was right at the window and completely visible to any passing trade. I was starting to feel some pain so also asked the delivery nurse who'd brought me up if she could bring me some Panadol. Ruby had still not had anything to drink but the nurse informed me it was not her job to look after me, all of those things would be taken care of now that I was back on the ward.

After gazing at my beautiful healthy baby I must have dozed because I was not sure how much time had passed. When I pressed my buzzer-call button no one appeared so I decided to have a shower. I started to get out of bed and my legs gave way beneath me. Whoops, I forgot about the epidural. I buzzed the call button again but there was still no sign of anyone. I managed to crawl back up into bed like I was escaping from Shawshank.

One by one women were being admitted to the ward and each time I would ask the nurse could I have a painkiller or what should I do with Ruby, but each one of them said they'd send a ward sister in. Still no one appeared. I was stuck in a loop of getting angry, pressing the buzzer then falling into a deep sleep. The baby hadn't fed since arriving eight hours before. It just didn't seem right.

I finally awoke to find Dan at my bedside nursing Ruby.

'What time is it?' I groggily enquired

'It's 5pm,' he said.

I told him that no one had come near us since the delivery nurse left me in the ward at 9 o'clock that morning. I had attempted to feed Ruby a few times but she wasn't latching on properly and I was in too much pain to sit up and hold her. Dan looked like he was going to hit the roof when I told him that I had fallen while trying to make it to the shower and he was apoplectic when I said that I had been given nothing to eat.

You cannot believe what a mild-mannered man Dan is . . . except when his feathers are badly ruffled. Then, anyone who can't swim, grab a chair. He left the room in a fury and when he returned (still very angry) he told me the nurse had said there was nothing written up on the board indicating the bed I was in was occupied so when the buzzer kept going off they had thought it was a malfunction.

One would think the staff would spring into action with such an oversight but alas it was shift-change time again, so the next 'lot' would be in to sort me out as soon as they could. Dan ended up going to the local supermarket to get me Panadol and something to eat. When he returned he held the baby up to my arms and she started to feed properly for the first time in 15 hours. Poor little thing, she must have been starving.

There is not much of your dignity intact after you've given birth but you would like to think that the days when your husband has to shower you are still years away. In my case not.

Ruby was awake all through the night, set off by the other newbies in the room but I didn't care. I not only had the most beautiful baby in the world but the best husband ever.

The next morning I finally had a visit from an obstetrician (not the one who'd delivered Ruby) who told us we could go home. We waited to see a nurse but after three hours of no one coming near us we packed up our things and were about to make our way out of that 'place', when one of the nurses came in and gave us an almighty serve.

How dare we attempt to leave with the baby before the proper procedures were in place. The baby had not been washed at all and was still covered in blood. I had not seen the lactation consultant and various bits of paperwork had not been completed.

Close your eyes and imagine what sort of reply that nurse got from us both. I vented like I was a cloven-hoofed extra on *Buffy the Vampire Slayer*. We didn't hang around for her reply.

I had managed to survive labour and so had Ruby. But only just. I have now worked out why so many women love talking about the actual birth of their children. It is because the experience is so horrific that the least everyone can do is let them unburden about what they've been through. Kind of like a 'rite of your passage'.

It seems only women who wear hemp clothing and natural-fibre headscarves have easy birthing experiences. 'Oh Harmony just slid out in an hour.' This might seem a touch aggressive, but I want to kill them. 'Oh we are keeping Quell-Beth-knee's placenta in the freezer until she is old enough to bury the omelette we made with it.' Somebody save me.

As sore, as tired and as inexperienced as I was I knew that Ruby, Dan and I would be fine. Surely now that the labour part was over, bringing a baby home wouldn't be too difficult. Dan and I were intelligent, sensible people with no addictions (shoes don't count) and relatively sound mental health. We could handle anything a baby threw at us. Couldn't we?

10

Baby's Back in Town

One morning I could see blood from my cracked nipples soaking through my shirt. I thought, What in God's name happened to my incredibly glamorous life?

In such a short space of time I'd gone from Alexander McQueen crocodile-embossed leather pumps to imitation 'Skinny's Hideout' sheepskin slippers. The days of coordinating my stylish outfits were long gone. Nowadays if I had to go out of the house I would pop on my 'good' tracksuit pants. My life had changed and I am not entirely sure I was ready.

Those first few weeks were a blur of bottles, crying and nappies . . . and I'm not talking about the baby. The community midwives visited each day for the first two weeks to give me more conflicting information. By the third week I had such severe mastitis that I was delaying Ruby's feeds to avoid the searing pain.

When I'd been six months' pregnant, one of my many midwives suggested I prepare my nipples for breastfeeding by toughening them up with a toothbrush or a loofah. Yes, yes! I see now how it was the wrong thing to do but it sounded perfectly logical to me, and I love homework, so I got stuck into it. By the time Ruby was born I could have popped on a couple of areola clamps and dragged a jumbo across a tarmac they were so tough.

The worst part about all that scrubbing, breaking the capillaries and damaging my milk ducts, was that I DID IT TO MYSELF. And then, to top off the awfulness of the whole situation, I was told over and over by EVERYONE that it was much better to feed through the pain. (Better for who? I ask. Not for me, as I was in absolute agony, and definitely not for

Ruby, whose mother was gritting her teeth and wishing it was over as soon as she came near my breast. That's not how you bond with your baby.) Breast is best, *blah, blah, blah*. To avoid the 'shame' of not breastfeeding and being ostracised by the breast police, I continued feeding Ruby until I had an abscess the size of a kiwi fruit. Good job.

Not long before Ruby was born Dan had started working at the BBC and his two-week paternity leave flew by. Before I knew it he had to return to the grind. He'd leave home just after seven in the morning and get back just before eight at night. To say I was beside myself is an understatement. I was stuck way out on the outskirts of London with a new baby, broken hooters, no family and no support network nearby. I was tired, cranky, feeling ill and wishing someone could stop my breasts from aching. I'd catch glimpses of myself in the bathroom mirror and wonder who that dark-eyed creature with bed hair was. It seemed like only a minute ago that I was dancing on a table in Ibiza . . . Calling it the baby blues makes it seem so trivial. I had plenty to be dispirited about.

To top it all off one of my best girlfriends, Ingrid, was moving home to Australia. This was really confronting as we had been through so many of each other's ups and downs over the years. Not having her around was going to add to my loneliness. Becoming friends in the early '90s when Ingrid was managing the Comedy Store in Sydney, we had no idea that our friendship would include moves from Sydney to Melbourne and then to the UK. She was my confidante, and she was leaving.

The only thing keeping me sane was Ruby. What a little champion. She was a great sleeper and a sensational burper with a very happy disposition: the text-book perfect baby. If only she had a text-book perfect mother. But my breasts put paid to that. I ended up having to take Ruby with me to the hospital every second day for seven weeks to consult with the surgeon before having the abscess aspirated. (Lovely, I know.) I arrived at the hospital at 9am and I was able to leave by around 2pm. The 'good' tracksuit pants had just enough time to dry before each outing.

It was all just so much fun that I couldn't believe I hadn't had a baby sooner.

The most common newborn advice I received from close friends was along the lines of, 'Don't kill yourself in the first 12 weeks.' Okay good, great advice and it gave me a goal to achieve before surfacing out of the zombie town that is new parenthood. It would have been more advantageous if someone had said, 'Don't sit on the couch and eat cookies every time the baby is asleep for the first 12 weeks.' Now that would have helped me out a lot. I am sure I put back on all of my baby weight after Ruby was born.

I had the notion that the 12-week marker would restore me to my normal self, so I made plans to take Ruby on a three-week trip to Australia with stop-overs in LA each way to introduce her to family and friends. Ruby was such a little cruiser I didn't think there'd be any drama. Dan couldn't get that much time off but I told him I was happy to go alone so Ruby could finally spend more than an hour with my mum and meet Poppy and Uncle Brendan. The plan was for Dan to meet Ruby and I in LA for a few days on the trip back.

I now understand that when you are a new mum you have absolutely no concept of how much your brain is still attached to your old life. You see yourself as capable of doing all that you used to do. I was determined to be some sort of Zena Warrior Princess/ Super Mother able to do it all. In actual fact I was not even switched on enough to be Zena's donkey's chaff bag but I didn't let that detail stop me.

The 12-hour flight from Heathrow to LA was easy. It was a night flight, so Ruby slept the whole way. I snatched sleep and kept waking to find myself dribbling on the arm of the person next to me. The good thing about new motherhood is that people forgive you for deeds that normal people would not get away with. If anyone glared at me for snoring or dribbling I just manoeuvred Ruby into their line of sight and any anger evaporated immediately. Brilliant.

Los Angeles was its usual fabulous self but it was here that I started to realise I wasn't. This time there were no long lunches in Santa Monica, or mojitos by the Skybar pool. I tried to go shopping at the Grove but it was a disaster. (Have you ever attempted to try something on in a fitting room with a pram next to you? 'Fitting' is not the word I am thinking of.) And those mirrors were unforgiving. (Please refer back to the advice about not eating biscuits. If only I knew!)

After the success of our London–LA flight, I was disgustingly smug as I checked in for the LA–Sydney leg. It didn't take long for things to unravel and it dawned on me that heading across the world with a baby in tow was not going to be as easy as I'd thought.

Sure you get to go onboard first but did you know that travelling with an infant does not guarantee you a seat with a bassinette? If someone checks in online or before you on the day and requests it, then it's just a case of bad luck woman. There was no way I was leaving Ruby alone in a bassinette next to a stranger. The person booking me in chirpily advised there was an alternative. I was presented with what looked remarkably like a sports bag that I'd use for the gym. When it was unzipped it was supposed to magically transform into a baby bed but I am sorry, it still looked like a sports bag.

I had an aisle seat in the middle section and so the only place for the sports/sleeping bag was on the floor at my feet. After only six hours of the 14-hour flight I was so exhausted from lifting the bag out of the way every time someone came near it that I just put it down and crossed my fingers that the drinks trolley didn't roll over Ruby's head while I was tucking into the satisfying two-centimetre cubed bit of cheese that the flight attendant threw in my direction at about 4am. By the time we were ready to land I felt like a deranged, crumpled, sleep-deprived mess. You know those photos of celebrities without make-up, where they look bedraggled and defeated? Compared to how I looked after this flight they could have been on the Oscars red carpet!

Despite the fact I could barely keep my eyes open, I made sure I looked out of the window as we descended over Sydney. I don't think it matters where you are from or how many times you have done it, flying past the Harbour Bridge and the Opera House as the sun is rising (or at any other time) is absolutely breathtaking. It's as if the city is flirting with you before you have even touched down. Cheeky piece.

It was a very strange sensation to be back in Australia with my new little girl. So much had changed since I'd decided to try my luck overseas. Staying with Mum and Dad for three weeks was stupendous: it was like being at a baby masterclass with TLC and copious cuppas included. (TLC = Tender Loving Care, not some new party drug, just so we are clear.) Though it had been years since she'd had a tiny baby to look after, my mum just knew what Ruby and I needed.

As far as I am concerned mums are the superheroes of the homo sapiens species. (Dads are the best men on the planet but we all know mums are the gurus.) I only started to comprehend what a goddess my mother was in my late 20s and my deep admiration for her just grew from there. Once I had my own daughter I appreciated exactly how magnificent she is.

When you have a child of your own you start to get an inkling of what your mother and father sacrificed for you. At least I did. It blew my mind. What a shame there was no way of taking back all those angsty teenage moments I'd put them through. I guess karma will see it come back to me through Ruby. (God help me!)

Staying in my old room with a crib alongside my bed made me feel a bit like I was a teen-mum living at home, but I only needed to see the wrinkles and black circles under my eyes to remind myself I was certainly no teen!

I managed to fit in a few TV appearances while I was home, popping in to see Kerri-Anne (the fairy godmother of live TV) and I even made an appearance on Hillsy's *Spicks and Specks*. Now, I doubt you will be shocked to hear that I am not the greatest music expert in the world, but combine that with 12-week-old-baby-brain and you will find that being near me was like standing next to an open window, no lights on, and definitely no one home. Each time Adam asked a question I knew the answer for, I would buzz in with zeal but by the time (two seconds later) he said my name the answer had left my head. Sort of like:

'Oh, oh, I know, I know . . . hang on, aww, hang on, aww . . . Nah, no sorry it's gone.'

This happened about seven times in half an hour. I swear I know more than this performance hinted at . . . but you'll just have to take my word for that because we have no recorded evidence.

By the time three weeks blinked by I was feeling slightly more human and my body had actually stopped aching, even if my mind was still a void. But leaving Australia this time was like slicing off a bit of my heart. Homesickness had crept back into my bones. After nearly 18 years of travelling, partying, working and generally living *la vida loca*, even though Dan was delicious with his love and support back in London I felt like I was stuck somewhere I didn't want to be.

So many people said to me, 'Why don't you and Dan just pack up and go home?'

It sounded so easy but it was anything but. I didn't feel like I had achieved everything I set out to do in the UK. I tend to forget about the great things I've done and just focus on what I still wanted to do. As a stand-up comedian, you don't hear the 499 people laughing in the audience, you only see that one guy down the front who doesn't. That's how I thought of my career. The truth was I'd built a solid international reputation over the eight years I had lived in London so to turn my back on it all and return to Australia on the off-chance there may be some work was just too risky.

Then there was Dan. Australia was my home, not his. How could I ask him to say goodbye to his life in London to start a new one in another country? It would mean him leaving behind his family and his lifelong friends and I knew how hard that would be. It was much easier to stay put than to even begin to contemplate moving the three of us back to Australia. But sometimes fate has other ideas . . .

One morning in mid-May of 2007 I got a call from my Aussie agent with the most extraordinary offer. Ollie and Robyn had been my agents for four years, but we had been friends for about 14 years.

Ollie couldn't believe that the only thing keeping us from moving back to Australia was a job, so she got on the phone. As usual, whenever anything happens to me I can't wait to tell Dan. I called him at work straight away. 'Brian Walsh from Foxtel has offered to fly us out to Australia and put us up for five months so I can work on a show called *The Singing Office.* It sounds like a riot.' We talked about it and somehow the idea of Dan resigning from work and us spending the rest of the year in Australia became a possible plan. Dan had no great love for advertising and this was a really good opportunity.

I had worked for Brian many years before on various Foxtel projects (*Beauty and the Beast* being my favourite), so I knew I was going to be in good hands. I'd had various offers to host shows in Australia but no one had ever been willing to put their money where their mouths were and actually bring us out. Here was the chance for Dan to spend some time in Australia to see if he could live there. We ummed and aahhed, did our maths, and finally decided that it was worth the leap. Once the decision was made we had five weeks to pack up our lives and get ready to fly back to Oz.

What do you pack when you don't know how long you are going to be away? Travelling with a baby takes up most of your luggage allowance anyway – by the time you pack sterilisers, clothes, bottles and the whole catastrophe there is only space left for a couple of pairs of undies, your jeans and maybe a T-shirt. (Mummy comes last, remember?)

We flew via the States again to see family and friends and while we were in Walnut Creek, just across the bay from San Francisco, we passed a shoe shop called Foot Candy. The contents of the window were so overwhelmingly magnificent they were physically hurting my feelings. (I think I may have left some saliva on the door.)

There was one pair of shoes that caught my bedazzled eye more than any other. A sexy, cherry-red patent heel with a pointed toe and classic Mary Jane strap. Looking a little closer, I went all lightheaded as the label whispered back to me, 'Manolo Blahnik'.

Dan said casually, 'Why don't you go in and try them on?'

Sometimes men just don't get it. There was no way I could just go in and 'try them on', knowing full well we couldn't afford them. I would rather not know how they felt on, the way they would gently encase and caress the foot while elevating it, using years of Mr Blahnik's handmade master-craftsmanship to become the perfect shoe. I had to let them go but I knew I would never forget them from the first moment I saw them.

We finally arrived in Melbourne after a very long flight and headed straight to the serviced apartment in the Docklands that would become our home for the next few months. A film crew and make-up artist were waiting for us in our loungeroom and I was straight to work! (Sue the make-up artist was a true artist in every sense of the word as she went about hiding my jetlag-no-sleeping-mumma look.)

By the time I returned to the apartment a few hours later, I was cross-eyed with fatigue. The three of us were all ready for a family coma and, stumbling into bed, I couldn't help notice the box on my pillow.

'What's this?' I asked Dan.

'Open it,' he replied.

It was the red shoes.

'I thought you deserved them for getting your new job,' he said as I looked at him in amazement.

What a man!

(It was the exact same feeling of elated disbelief I had on Christmas morning in 1975 when I thought all our presents had been opened and then Mum said, 'Julia, there is still one more for you' and there she was, hiding in the corner, Rub-a-Dub Dolly. *Bliss.*)

Things were really looking up. I'd somehow made the transition from tracky-daks to red Manolos. Mummy/Julia was back!

Making *The Singing Office* was so much fun. The idea of the show was that my fellow team leader, the ultra-charming Gus Worland, and I would go into offices and surprise people at their desks by asking them to sing us a song. Choosing a final five, we would then whisk them off to have two days of intensive singing and dancing rehearsals, then they would compete against another company for a place in the grand final.

I loved the show but it was very intense going from stay-at-home mummy to working for ten hours a day five days a week. I was shattered. At the same time Dan was going through his own baptism of fire. He'd gone from full-time work to full-time stay-at-home dad. Each night when I would arrive home physically and emotionally drained from a big day of showbiz, Dan would already have Ruby bathed and fed, and be ready to put our dinner on the table. He was proving a much better mum than me. He didn't seem to struggle with the transition at all and we were a very happy family unit.

The show had a filming break of ten weeks before the grand final was scheduled, so we decided to spend the hiatus on the beach on the glorious New South Wales Central Coast, where I had grown up. For a Welshman who had spent most of his adult life in London, Dan took to the 'sea change' with ease. He'd make time to head out surfing each day, taught Ruby to swim and told me he could not believe his luck to have such an amazing ten-week beach holiday. Then there was the final filming and our return to the reality of the UK winter.

With our holiday drawing to a close, we were shaking the sand from everything, ready to pack up and head back down to Melbourne, when Dan said, 'What are we doing living in London?' It was a question I couldn't answer. We had both fallen in love with our new Australian life and the luxury associated with getting to spend so much time together as a family with Ruby.

Then, like 'the dawning of the Age of Aquarius', all our planets aligned and Ollie called me with the possibility of a new show. My inner sirens went off when she said, 'It's not so much a reality show, it's more like a talent quest . . .'

Oh, no!

She then explained it was a Channel 7 production called *It Takes Two* in which I would be partnered with an Australian singing star and compete each week against other 'celebrities'. The audience would ring in each week and vote to keep me around.

Oh *nooooooooooo*!

It is impossible to know how you will be perceived by the nation when you compete on a show like that. As a seasoned (sounds like chicken!) stand-up I have been a solo performer for many years but I always had the advantage of the 'fourth wall'. (The fourth wall is an imaginary barrier between you and the audience, which means you can control how much the audience gets to see. On a show like this all safety barriers would be down and I would be completely exposed.)

I had never seen this particular program but I'd seen shows like *Big Brother*, so the whole concept terrified me. I was scared I'd accidentally 'leak' some dreadful hidden quality I didn't even know I had and that would be the end of me and any semblance of a career. Goodbye comedy work.

I didn't know what to do. On one hand it could become my worst nightmare but on the other hand it was a paying job and a lifeline that would allow us to come back to Australia for three more months.

We decided to return to London and make our decision there.

The nine-day lead-up to Christmas in LA gave us time to really talk about what we should do about *It Takes Two*. I asked my agent to ring Brian Walsh and make sure I had his blessing, as he had been the one to make the original investment of bringing us out to Australia, so it was thanks to him that I received this new offer. The blessing came through so we headed off to the UK knowing it would be for only a month. I was going to say yes to Channel 7.

Touching down in Heathrow doesn't have quite the same majesty as touching down in Sydney. (The flight path seldom takes you up the Thames past 'Buck' Palace and the Houses of Parliament, more's the pity.)

We were only back in England for two days before Ruby came down with a vomiting/poo poo flu that was so bitterly hostile and so contagious that the news reports on every network were urging anyone who had contracted it to stay away from doctors and hospitals to contain its spread. Our poor little chooky was so violently ill and we were beside ourselves because we couldn't do anything to make her better other than keep her clean and hydrated. It had to run its course.

Knowing we were only back for a month we had made lots of plans, including travelling to Wales to see Dan's family, then attending the wedding of two very close friends in the southwest of England. After that we were heading back to London to see friends before sorting out our wordly possessions and getting ready to fly back to Australia.

We missed the lot. The virus was just as contagious as the news reports had warned, so Dan and I went down like a ton of bricks. All three of us were so very sick that we did not make it out to do anything. No friends, no family, no nothing. Once we stopped vomiting it was agonisingly frustrating to lie around lethargically, not even able to find the energy to change the TV channel. Before we knew it, it was time to leave. I talked Dan into staying an extra week so he could at least see some of his family and friends. All in all, the trip back to the

UK had been an expensive disaster and I couldn't wait to return to the sun, leaving the leaden skies of London far behind.

By the time Dan followed Ruby and I back to Australia it was only days away from the first day of filming. Once it began we would be commuting from Avoca to Melbourne each week. It seemed just too silly to come back to Australia and not be close to Mum and Dad (and to have a babysitter we could trust was a luxury we couldn't refuse) so we decided to make our temporary home on the coast. The drive from there to Sydney Airport took longer than the flight to Melbourne and I just crossed my fingers that a bushfire or dropped truck load didn't close the F3 freeway and make the trip almost impossible. But the best thing was we were worlds away from Woodside Park, and the beach was a short walk away so we embraced it all.

I mentioned the red shoes and Rub-a-Dub Dolly earlier on, but they were nothing in comparison to how I felt when I learned I was to be paired with the supreme opera star David Hobson. What do you get when you cross a comedian with an opera singer? You get two, all-time funsters who can't stop laughing long enough to get any singing practice done! I had been concerned that David might be too conservative to have any fun but it turned out that I was the conservative one.

Not knowing how long we would last in the series, I booked in as much comedy work as I could fit in between the shows. Dan, Ruby and I became like some sort of gypsy caravan.

It was a crazy life. Sunday and Monday were rehearsal days in Melbourne; Tuesday was show day; then Wednesday morning was spent learning the next week's song if we made it through.

In Week One we sang an old Gloria Estefan song I had loved for years, 'Everlasting Love'. We did alright for a first attempt. The next day Dan, Ruby and I were off to Byron Bay for the Bangalow Comedy Festival. Dan was still enjoying 'daddy daycare' and I couldn't have stretched myself so thin without him creating such a solid, uncomplaining support base.

Back on Week Two of the show meant some hard work having to reach the high notes in the Motown classic, Aretha Franklin's 'Think'. I kept calling her Urethra Franklin but I have a feeling I was the only one laughing. (Business as usual!)

After only two weeks on air I was starting to be more and more recognised when I was out and about. It was lovely to know people were watching and liking the show. My fears started to melt a little. People kept asking me for my voting phone number and I couldn't remember it for love or money. I came up with a scathingly brilliant idea and asked a friend of mine from Richardson's Jewellers in Queensland to make me a necklace not unlike the one made famous by Carrie Bradshaw (aka SJP) in *Sex and the City.* Instead of my name in gold I wanted my voting number in gold. It was the best thing I had ever seen (okay, after Dan, Ruby, the red shoes and my Rub-a-Dub Dolly). It was so big that when I put it on, it looked like I was wearing a really glamorous prison number!

Week Three of *It Takes Two* proved an altogether more serious affair with David and I singing 'Don't

Cry Out Loud'. My man-maid Juzzy had been singing me that song for about ten years, replacing words to make me laugh. So every time David and I sang it, all I could hear in my head was 'baby cried the day the funbags came to town . . .'. As they say on these types of shows, it was such a rollercoaster-challenge-journey. I was loving every minute of it.

As soon as episode three was in the can I headed off with Dan and Ruby to do a show in Townsville and then back to Melbourne for the annual 'March for Melanoma', held by the charity I had chosen to support for the show. I'd had a melanoma removed when I was 21 and another one just recently so it seemed only natural to nominate a charity like the Emily Tapp Foundation, which promotes skin cancer awareness and prevention. After a typical beachside/poolside baking childhood around Gosford I was not alone in ignoring the dangers of too much sun. In both my cases, early detection was the key to recovery. If only Emily had been awarded that same luxury. I hoped that I could help make a difference to someone else's life by raising money for the cause.

Week Four came around really fast and David and I knew as soon as we performed that we hadn't set the studio alight. 'Reet Petite' was the rock 'n' roll gem we churned out but the real news was that I was four weeks' pregnant. We were overjoyed but, considering my past history, Dan and I decided to keep it to ourselves for a few more weeks (this time I managed to keep the secret . . . mostly). I was already showing visible signs of being tired but I could easily explain that by pointing out the commuting and extra touring I was doing. A part of me wondered how on earth I was going to manage it all, but I just had to forge on.

By that stage of the show David and his superlative wife, Amber, had welcomed us into their home like we were old friends. Amber and Dan would sit together for each filming giggling and cheering, then give David and I a proper critique at the end. With the two of them heading up 'Team D-Ho and J-Mo' (we shortened it during Mardi Gras to 'Team Ho-Mo'), each week Amber and Dan swung into action sending reminders to everyone we knew to vote (for us).

In Week Five Dan and I told David and Amber our baby news. They were so delighted for us and did everything they could to make sure I was not feeling too spent. Of course that was the week I had to get into a Tina Turner wig, mini skirt and heels to match David's 'Mad Max' while we sang 'We Don't Need Another Hero'. Could my life get any more surreal?

If I'd known I was going to be pregnant during my show at the Melbourne International Comedy Festival I might not have accepted so much work. Every week on *It Takes Two* was a shock and a delight that we'd made it through, but I hadn't expected to get that far. Combining the TV work with the festival show meant my energy levels started depleting rapidly.

I didn't have much morning sickness with Ruby, maybe a week or so, but this new baby had me feeling quite queasy much of the time. You can imagine how delighted I was with the dance rehearsals and being spun around. For Week Six David and I decided to rest up a little and cover a much more sedate number with 'No More Tears (Enough is Enough)'. (I got to be the Barbra.) The one judge's comment I do remember from that night was, 'You could have done with a lot more dancing.' I thought, but didn't say, 'You could have done with a protective raincoat if I did!'

By Week Seven I had to confide in Val, the guru of television stylists, that my belly was on the move in an outwards direction. Val and I had been friends since my old *Full Frontal* days so I knew my secret was safe. Using her wardrobe wizardry she managed to come up with gowns each week that hid my ever-increasing bump. Let's just say the woman has supernatural powers over garments.

I can't speak about Week Eight without getting a little dose of the cringes. The hairdo I sported for 'The Rose' made me look like a Bette Midler impersonator in drag. The song was not much better but we were saved with our rendition of John Denver's gem 'Grandma's Feather Bed'. I am ashamed to admit to you that I didn't have to learn it, I knew it word for word. David and I maintain, even to this day, that 'Feather Bed' was our favourite song of the whole series.

Each time I'd arrive home from filming I'd regale Dan and Ruby (when she wasn't otherwise engaged with Dora the Explorer) with backstage stories. When we weren't all travelling together from one gig to another like some carny family, I loved nothing more than coming home to them.

Since the beginning of the series all I had ever hoped for (though I didn't think I'd get there) was making it to Week Nine, when we had to sing in the genre of our partner and, let's face it, who doesn't want to hear me sing opera? The only way I knew I would get away with it was by taping some saucepan lids to my knees and banging them while singing the beautiful aria the '*Habanera*' from *Carmen*.

This is the best example of what an A-grade superstar David Hobson really is. Revered by peers, with a voice like liquid silk, D-Ho rose to the occasion and let it rip. I am sure many highbrow opera eyes would have been on him but David threw himself into the silliness. It takes an artist of pure quality to mentor another performer enough to let them shine while taking very little of the glory for themselves. He is pure gold.

When asked by the cheeky host Grant Denyer to look down the barrel of the camera and make a case to viewers as to why I should be put into the grand final of the show, I could only say, 'I think it's about time that an over-40, overweight woman won something in this country.'

No one was more shocked and delighted than David and I that we did make it to the grand final. By then I was so tired that I had to lie down between each rehearsal just to make it through but there was no way I wouldn't give it my best shot.

Choosing the songs for each show had been nearly as much work as the shows themselves. The problem was that this was the third series of *It Takes Two* so most of the great songs had already been done. With such slim pickings, we were lucky to even get some of our favourites. The hardest song to choose, though, was our 'journey' song. It was meant to reflect how the time on the show had affected us on an emotional level. Please, can you bear it? Show me a song that is all about the relief of ten weeks' wages and I will sing my heart out but otherwise it just seemed a bit forced.

I made a suggestion to David and we bounced it off the producers. After much discussion and back and forth yes's and no's we finally got the green light.

So, on 22 April 2008, two days after my 40th birthday and ten weeks' pregnant, David Hobson and I won the third series of *It Takes Two* singing our 'journey' song, Queen's 'Fat Bottomed Girls'.

I was in a daze as they announced our names and all I could think of was that my shoes had started to feel like razor blades, but we did it. The only other thing I had ever won was a first ribbon in Year 7 for Ball Games (make of that what you will) so this was just too much to take in all at once.

Once I came down from the euphoria of being a 'winner', the realities of life had to be dealt with. Dan and I were loving being in Australia and the fact that he was spending so much time with Ruby was priceless. We decided to stay and make a go of it. (The thought of delivering another child in the UK hospital system was more than enough to sway our decision.) The fabulous thing about putting myself out there in *It Takes Two* meant that people offered me gigs and came to my shows. It was stupendous to settle back into the showbiz groove in a place that had been so good to me for so long. I was baaaaack . . . and lovin' it.

Now I find when I am out in the streets people don't say to me, 'I know who you used to be' – they say, 'Hey, I loved you on *Dancing with the Stars*'. Mmm.

Don't you know who I used to be? is one of the more hilarious catchphrases I have been using for years. Back then it was a bit of a giggle about my 'C grade' status. But as I have relaxed more and more into the rhythms of having Ruby in my life, I started to realise that 'Don't you know who I used to be?' was completely relevant to motherhood and has nothing to do with celebrity.

Nearly every mum I have spoken to feels the same way in that first six to twelve months. You lose your identity and the sense of self that has defined you for such a long time. Moving out of the centre of your own world takes a lot of getting used to and to some extent it is like you are a hostage to this little person. Surrendering to that loss of self and the desire to nurture someone else is the key to mothering. It's not an easy thing to do and it is why I know my mother is a goddess. I hope one day Ruby feels that way about me. Any sadness about losing my old self has passed (getting out of the trackies was a good start) because I know I have an even larger, fuller life. You can't help it when you stop focusing on yourself.

That cross on a stick did change my life. No matter what happens I know who I am . . . I'm Ruby's mum.

P.S. And Sophie's (she slid out at Gosford District Hospital on 27 November 2008). But that's another story . . .

Acknowledgments

Maureen and Michael Morris; Brendan Morris; Graham Thomas; Marge Wilson; Trish and Mike Newman; Justin Miller; Ingrid Ricciardello; Michael Idato (my TV sat-nav); Jules and Crispin Leyser; TV's Carolyn Ashton; Benn Haitsma; Angus Malcolm; Ben and Colin Nash; Brodie Lane; Bryan Scott; Christopher Price; Sally Judd and International Artists; Jon Plowman; Emma Turner; Jena Girouard; Eddy and Jane Cassar; Brian Walsh; Fraser Smith; Graham Burrells, Caroline Spencer, Maurice Parker and the Foxtel team; Felicity Brown; Angel Eye; Janette Linden and PBJ Management; Peter Bennett-

Jones; Geoffrey Perkins; Jill Peacock; David and Amber Hobson; Lisa Fitzpatrick and the Channel 7 team; Julie Ward; everyone who voted for us on *It Takes Two*; Amanda Fry and the 6DC team; Hachette Australia for giving me the best editor in publishing – the goddess Vanessa Radnidge; and, last but by certainly no means least, my dear friends Ollie Simon and Robyn McCoy from Star 100 Entertainment, without whom I would still be living on the outskirts of London in the rain.

Thank you all for your love and support.